raymond morineau

lebanon today

88 colour photographs
14 maps and circuits

éditions jeune afrique

lebanon
today

summary

6 **panorama**

town by town 86

lebanese journey 167

panorama

*Children like these little girls of Sidon are not in the least impressed
by the remains of the past — there are so many of them!
(Photo F. Roiter.)*

Previous page: *The imposing ruins of the temple of Jupiter at
Baalbek seen against Mount Lebanon covered with snow.
(Photo NCT.)*

man and the soil

Lebanon is, above all, a name which arouses memories. Memories of the Bible, literary memories, and the somewhat mysterious resonance of these two syllables full of a strange Oriental rustic poetry. Goats, mountains, milk and whiteness...

The Arabic word *Lebnan* is derived from an Aramaic word meaning white. The whiteness of mountains covered with snow until springtime, the whiteness of milk — *halib* in Lebanese Arabic and *laban* in Egyptian Arabic (a word which, in Lebanon, means curdled milk).

So close to and impregnated by old Europe that it no longer attributes much importance to her — perhaps justifiably so — Lebanon, by the very sound of its name, seems to be a far-off country shrouded in the mists of history and legend. And yet, the State which bears this name is not even fifty years old. Here is a first contrast, the forerunner of many others.

A very young old country

The country of the Song of Songs is today one of the most sophisticated financial and trading centres of the world. From Beirut, the chattering teletypes unceasingly send messages to all the capitals of the planet — purchase of goods in Tokyo for re-sale in Buenos Ayres, without the Lebanese businessman who conducts this triangular operation ever setting eyes on the object of the transaction. This is pure broking — or impure — it depends on your point of view. It is, in any case, a pioneering technique in modern commercial practice.

Businessman and pleasure-seeker, the well-to-do Lebanese is proud of the black-marble commercial centres of Beirut bursting with luxury products, the first-class hotels with obsequious waiters opening glass doors, the private beaches, the beautiful, elegant women, the fast cars and motor-boats, and the stakes played for at the Casino, just as he is of his air-conditioned offices, his financial competence, his swift, sure decisions, his "American businessman" outlook and his ability to speak three or four foreign languages.

But every week-end this same man returns to his winter-sports chalet or his mountain retreat situated in a changeless landscape which has not yet been polluted by urban civilization or made hideous by concrete, among a population which, even more than that of Beirut, has retained the virtues of hospitality, dignity and even nobility of a very old people in all their moving authenticity.

Lebanon is a mountain

For the child who is fond of maps and engravings, Lebanon is the former Phoenicia — a country of the sea and one which, long before Britannia and for much longer, ruled the waves. But the city-states of this people of Canaan, who may well have derived their name from the purple-dye industry, only formed leagues and alliances between one another, often fought one another, but practically never took any interest in the mountain whose insistent presence imposes itself as far as the coast.

Yet Lebanon is the name of a mountain. This country does not owe its name to a people as do England, France, Germany and Turkey, or to a man like America, or to its geographical situation like Japan. No, Lebanon is a mountain. Nor does geography contradict such an identification, for Lebanon owes its unity to this mountainous nucleus almost entirely contained within its frontiers. Visitors to the Beirut National Museum, who study attentively the vast model showing the relief of the country, find themselves obliged to reject the artificial reproach made against the

In the Bekaa peaceful shepherds lead huge herds of sheep to pasture. (Photo NCT.)

creation of Lebanon by those who are in favour of a "Greater Syria".

A small country

With an area of only 10,400 km2, 210 km long from north to south and from 40 to 75 km in width from east to west, Lebanon looks, on a map of the Mediterranean, like a small window in the almost straight wall made up of the coasts of Anatolia, Syria, Lebanon, Palestine and Egypt.

Broadly speaking, the Lebanese territory consists of four distinct parts:

— a very narrow coastal plain, which was the cradle of the Phoenician maritime civilization;

— a mountain range running from north to south, Mount Lebanon which covers more than a third of the country and whose western slopes, covered with greenery and frequently broken by beautiful, picturesque valleys, rise gradually over a distance of some thirty kilometres to the highest peaks of the country (Sannine: 2,628 metres and Kornet es-Saouda: 3,068 metres), whereas its arid eastern slopes fall abruptly;

— the Bekaa plateau from 8 to 15 km wide also running from north to south over a distance of 120 km at an average height of 1,000 metres;

— and the western flank of the Anti-Lebanon and the Hermon, a chain of almost deserted mountains, again running from north to south and forming the frontier between Lebanon and Syria.

Even this rough division provides evidence of that diversity, within such narrow limits, which is an essential characteristic of Lebanon. If to this geographical diversity, which is manifested by an even greater variety in scenery, we add the extraordinary concentration of archaeological and historical wealth of a region which has so often been invaded and has been the melting-pot of so many civilizations, we come to the conclusion that nowhere else in the world is so much natural beauty and so much human, archaeological and historical interest concentrated in such a small area,

The modern port of Saida, which used to be Sidon. Do these
young Lebanese remember that the Phoenicians left on their
distant voyages from here and that Louis, the French king who
crossed himself twice, had this fortress built?
(Photo Almasy.)

accompanied by such a climate, such pure air and such a rich variety of vegetation.

Lebanese customs

Anyone, therefore, who really knows Lebanon can only be annoyed at the insistence of so many travel agencies on sending visitors only to Beirut and allowing them only a few organized trips to the famous places. Lebanon should be seen lovingly, long and lazily, stopping from time to time to drink the cool water of the springs, abandoning oneself to the sun while sitting on the fallen column of a ruined Roman temple, under the pines of Cilicia on the Qammoua plateau, or on a rock near Jezzine where the lizards bask themselves, or under the greenery and awnings of those adorable cafés which spring up along the water's edge and round the springs.

Lebanon is not Beirut, no matter how large and voracious the capital may be. Although the inhabitants still remain attached to the mountain and may well nourish within themselves a vague nostalgia for the joy it gave them when they were children, they can only give the visitor a deformed image of Lebanon. In this vast, cosmopolitan city, business, money, material success and concern for standing sometimes seem to make the authentic qualities of the Lebanese people recede into the background, although these qualities can still be found intact in the mountains. Undoubtedly, there still are people in a small way at Beirut who have not lost the virtues of the mountain-dweller, just as there are a number of well-to-do people who have miraculously managed to combine ancestral qualities with an up-to-date attitude. It is in the mountains that we find that natural, spontaneous outlook, that warm sympathy for everything which is just human. It is in some wild

A tidal wave of concrete is submerging Ras Beirut, the most advanced point on the Lebanese coast. (Photo NCT.)

village that a visitor interested in the making of *marqouq*, the mountain bread, will be offered one or two loaves, by a man carrying a rifle and covered with cartridge pouches, or that he will be shown the way by boys without the least thought of reward and only expecting sincere thanks and a smile of gratitude.

The ever-present mountain

The narrow twisting strip of coastal plain is unceasingly threatened and even severed by the invading mountain. At two points the haughty rock advances as far as the sea, compelling the road to go underground - once, at the small tunnel of Nahr al-Kalb 15 km from Beirut, and once at the larger tunnel of Ras Chekka 9 km south of Chekka, a small town covered with the dust from three cement-works. Whereas in the neighbourhood of Tripoli and to the east of the town, the mountain keeps its distance, abandoning the vast Koura plain to a sea of olive-trees — a sudden blossoming after the savage character of the Kadisha valley upstream.

Between Tripoli and Batroun, the traveller's eyes wandering from the green slopes of the hills to the eternal sea, come to rest on the salt marshes dotted with windmill pumps which, for mile after mile, form a complicated puzzle of checkered emerald pools with here and there the dazzling whiteness of a small heap of salt. But a dozen kilometres south of Tripoli, he could have seen, towering over the proudest peak in the area, the magnificent Abbey of Balamend, founded by the Cistercians in the thirteenth century and occupied since 1289 by orthodox monks who enjoy a fantastic view of both land and sea.

The narrow plain which then runs along the coast has only a poor vegetation, suddenly blossoming out as it comes to the mouth of a river,

*Glass-blowing — a thousand-year old industry which goes back
to when the Phoenicians were under the artistic influence
of the Egyptians — still goes on in three workshops at Sarafand,
Batroun and near Tripoli.
(Photo M. Guillard.)*

The Lebanon is a mountain with varied aspects. Near the coast the landscape is very Mediterranean in type. (Photo M. Guillard.)

which is nearly always crossed, not far from the coast, by an old Roman or Arab bridge surrounded by bullrushes. The valley of the Nahr ej-Jauz leads to the dark dungeon of Mseilha. After Batroun, the coast becomes gayer and the orchards denser. There is a wealth of pretty little creeks and tiny harbours. Batroun itself (the former Bothrys), the lemonade town (all the cars stop on each side of the main street and small boys come running up with trays full of the famous drink) still has its old harbour and its silent streets of mysterious, old Arab houses.

But the mountain unceasingly imposes itself, providing a very near horizon and extending its rocky foot to the shore. The coastal plain from Beirut to Tripoli is nothing but a succession of tiny plots of greenery interspersed with arid stretches and dominated by heights some of which are soft with their covering of green pines and oak-trees, while others are dry and rocky.

The triumph of the orchards

South of Beirut, once the miserable slums into which the coastline crowned by the proud buildings of Ras Beirut has degenerated have been left behind, the coastal plain consists of a series of orchards the richness of which increases the further south we go. And yet, from time to time, the bare mountain thrusts aggressively out to the coast, for in the southern half of Lebanon, except in the mouths of the rivers, particularly the Damour and the Litani, it nearly always has a dry and desert look.

But the richness of the orchards of orange, lemon, apricot, fig and peach-trees, and the green tides of the banana-trees with their huge slashed leaves lying between the road and the sea in which they appear to float, are quite different from the modest cultivation of the northern coastal plain.

*Lebanon, proud of its fine fruit swollen by the sun, presents
the rich, pleasant orchards of Kesrouane for the admiration
of visitors.
(Photo NCT.)*

Here, the grand houses, which one can only guess to be particularly luxurious, are hidden behind walls and curtains of cypress-trees. In contradistinction to the rural opulence of the wealthy properties which recall the Roman *latifundia*, the villages appear to be less well cared for, less flowery and more swarming. And the mountain, not so high as in the north after the fine wooded slopes of the Chouf, allows the naked chalk rock more and more frequently to appear in a savagely desolate countryside.

The changing landscape

Lebanon has been called the Switzerland of the Middle East, and if Switzerland is the synonym of mountain this is true. But the western part of Mount Lebanon is a Mediterranean mountain with specifically Lebanese contrasts. Over a distance of 200 kilometres from north to south there is a prodigious variety of scenery.

In the north, the dark, savage Akkar softens out into the delicious calm of the Qammoua Plateau, a vast meadowland surrounded by water sources, and then goes on through a broken line of hills covered with apple-trees to a height of 1,200 metres in the Danniye region, while to the east the yellow line of bare peaks announces the desolation of the high mountains, the most characteristic expression of which is Kornet es-Saouda, the highest peak in Lebanon (3,088 m).

A little further south, there is the valley of the Kadisha, which varies between vertical, rocky falls and pleasant slopes covered with pine-trees and orchards tumbling joyfully down to villages nestling in greenery. Further on, after caza Jbail, the horizon broadens out on landscapes illustrating the eternal, but brotherly, rivalry between man and the aridity of a chalky soil, the enormous white outcrops of which seem to be unceasingly proclaiming their victory over the invasion of terraces of fig-trees, mulberries and nut-trees. This is a sort of compromise between the desert and the mountain. But now, suddenly, greenery appears again, the savage gorges with their vertiginous winding roads and the shores of the Nahr Ibrahim, the river of Adonis.

In the centre of the country, the mountain becomes less forbidding, with the Kesrouan, the Metn and even the Chouf. Without surrendering any of its picturesque grandeur, it often becomes generous and provides nourishment for fruit-trees and crops. Here we find a summer holiday centre every few kilometres; they become more or less fashionable every year in accordance with the vagaries of snobbery.

South Lebanon is very much less generous. At a lower elevation and more arid, it often provides nothing but bare rocky landscapes, and though these are not lacking in grandeur, they sometimes weigh heavily on the soul. But even here, the valley of the Litani audaciously cuts a heroic, headlong passage, best seen from the Castle of Beaufort, spreading on its narrow shores the benefits from its water and bringing back, only 35 km from the frontier, the luxuriant vegetation which appeared to have been abolished.

Water, source of life

Beirut lacks water. Volney remarked on this as much as 190 years ago. And this is one of the contrasts of which Lebanon is made up, for it seems that there is water everywhere in this small country. The south of the Bekaa is full of it. On a map of Lebanon, the word *Aïn* (spring) and its synonym *Nabeh* are undoubtedly found more frequently than any others. This water which trickles from the arid flanks of the mountain just as it does from

*There is water everywhere in Lebanon. Springs and waterfalls
in the mountains.
(Photo NCT.)*

Formerly, the high Lebanese mountain was covered with cedars, the hard and imperishable wood of which was coveted by the Phoenicians' neighbours. Although the forest has been decimated, the noble trees that remain are a symbol and the pride of Lebanon.
(Photo NCT - Yetenegian.)

the slopes covered with green pines and oak-trees, the object of religious veneration in former times, is the life blood of Lebanon. But it is blood which is being lost, as was that which flowed from the mortal wound of Adonis.

The cultivation of thousands of acres depends on a rational use of the water of these innumerable springs which impart to this country the idyllic aspect of the landscapes celebrated in Greek lyric poetry. They have to be tapped and domesticated. This was always done on an artisan scale, but a daring agricultural policy, together with the necessary technical resources, would enable it to be done on a technological basis.

The Ministry of Agriculture's "Green Plan" and the Litani project which is now being implemented constitute only a beginning. Meanwhile, the cemented irrigation channels of Kesrouan and Metn, and the little earth channels of the Akkar, which are moved in accordance with the farmer's requirements, make it possible to grow apples, oranges, lemons and figs. And meanwhile, at the foot of waterfalls, at the edge of natural basins, and in the neighbourhood of small and powerful springs (from the one at Nabeh Safah, two enormous bubbling jets spout out as though from a high-pressure main), these charming restful cafés and restaurants, some of them enormous, have sprung up, full of freshness and shade, so pleasant for both inhabitants of and visitors to Beirut.

The mountain refuge

Secretly, with welcoming arms, the Lebanese mountain, frequently divided up by delicious valleys going right up to the highest peaks and pierced with a vast number of caves, used to offer a peaceful haven to the seagoing people of the coast where was established the series of famous

*The Phoenicians had studded the coast with ports, the famous
names of which, such as Byblos, have a nostalgic ring in our ears.
(Photo Marinier.)*

harbours of antiquity — Tyre, Sidon, Beryte, Byblos, Bothrys and Aradus — each of which was a day's sailing from the next. And yet the Phoenicians, those Canaanites who mingled with the sea peoples, turned their backs on this mountain. These Semitic peoples who came from the desert mistrusted the obscure threatening mass which seemed to conceal its broken relief under mysterious contrasts.

The many invaders who, in ancient times, swept down from the Asian continent onto this tiny prosperous region with its charming climate — the Hurrites, Amorites, Hittites, Aramaeans, Chaldeans, Babylonians, Medes, Persians and Assyrians — like the invaders from the south, the Egyptians, and those who came from the sea, the Greeks and Romans, intermingled freely with the population, whereas the most resolute elements fled and took refuge in the mountain, which had been inhabited from time immemorial.

Thus Lebanon, from ancient times, discovered its vocation as a mountain refuge, the redoubt of the irreducibles, the most oustanding of whom, after the Arab conquest of the seventh century, were the Maronites, Christians who, in the first instance, took refuge in the valley of the Kadisha, the Holy Valley. The Franks, at the time of the Crusades, were well received by them and built their castles in the mountain itself as well as on the seashore.

When the liberal and tolerant rule of the Arabs during the first centuries of Islam was replaced by the brutal repression of the Mamelukes, the mountain constituted an enormous and constant centre of resistance against the latter.

All those in Lebanon, from antiquity until 1860, who diverged from the official doctrines, took refuge in the mountain, grouping themselves into a

A sumptuous town of antiquity, the excavations of which give some
idea of its grandeur, succeeded to the proud Tyre of Phoenicia.
A partial view of the Roman necropolis, with second century
sarcophaguses.
(Photo NCT.)

vast number of Christian, Moslem and Druze communities who usually got on well together, though from time to time they cut each other's throats under the pressure of dissension or rivalry, usually fomented from outside.

Unparalleled archaeological wealth

The archaeologist Maurice Dunand discovered at Byblos extensive remains going back to the neolithic and post-neolithic. The Amorites left considerable remains which had been covered by Babylonian and Egyptian buildings and ruins, before the complex features of Phoenician civilization, better known from the writings of neighbouring peoples than from their buildings, became apparent; and these were partially or completely destroyed by subsequent civilizations which raised other buildings on their ruins — Greek, Roman, Byzantine and Arab.

In spite of this "vertical" structure of Lebanese archaeology, the vestiges of the past are innumerable. It is difficult to go a mile in this country without catching a glimpse of the past, usually in the form of old stones but also in that of legends or natural sites venerated from time immemorial. In particular, the wealth of Roman temples in Lebanon is considerable. They have very often been transformed into Byzantine churches and then into mosques.

Some convents and churches still in use incorporate the foundations of Roman temples. The Crusaders chopped off the columns and used the stones of these buildings to fortify the walls of their castles. Many a peasant's house, too, is built with the debris from ancient monuments such as the Phoenician temple at Echmoun. These ruins fit harmoniously into the landscape and constitute one of the most typical features of Lebanon.

*At Saida, the Sea Castle built by the Crusaders rises from an
island a few cable lengths from the modern town.
(Photo NCT.)*

A centuries—old simple life is still carried on in the regions of the interior. The peasants still make "mountain bread", known as "markouk", which you fold like a cloth.
(Photo M. Guillard.)

An inextricable mixture

Few peoples are the result of such an inextricable mixture as the Lebanese. To the multitude of ancient peoples who spread out through the coastal and mountain areas of what was to become, several thousands years later, the Lebanese State — and even about these Canaanites of whom the Phoenicians formed a branch not very much is known — there were added, in more recent times, a whole lot of other elements, the most important of which, the Arabs, gave Lebanon its language and left the deepest mark on its civilization. But we should not forget the Crusaders, the Turks and, even more recently, the Armenians. How was it possible for a Lebanese type and a Lebanese mentality to emerge from such a mixture spread over so many centuries? Mysterious alchemy of the birth of a Nation! The accustomed eye succeeds in recognizing a Lebanese by his features. And yet, while the majority of Lebanese are dark-haired and dark-eyed, blonds and even redheads (there are lots of redheaded children in the village of Mechmech in the Akkar) with blue or, more frequently, green eyes are by no means rare. In fact, physically, the Lebanese man and woman correspond fairly well to the Westerner's idea of an Oriental when such "Orientality" is discreet.

As for mentality, since the conditions of life in Beirut are so vastly different from those in the mountain fastnesses, this is difficult to define. There is a temptation to attribute to the city-dwellers alone the love and aptitude for business dealings inherited from the Phoenicians. But now and again, the brilliant success of some mountain-dweller who has emigrated to Brazil or the United States proves that such faculties are latent in nearly all Lebanese and bear witness to a very widespread agility of mind. Willingness to help, sense of hospitality, but also the need to "show off", that other aspect of the dignity and sense of honour which govern the conduct of the mountain people — all these features to a greater or less degree, can be found in the Lebanese character.

Individualism and the car

While closely attached to the manners and customs of his community, and therefore, from this point of view, conformist, the Lebanese is extremely individualist. His individualism essentially consists in the rejection of the discipline imposed on everybody. This is his way of asserting himself, of getting himself taken into consideration, of showing he is not just anybody. His behaviour as a car-driver is the most striking illustration of his individualism.

Driving a car in Lebanon is more a matter of fantasy and virtuosity than of rules and regulations. Once the visitor has understood that, things become clear. For example, along the middle of the road there are unbroken white lines which must not be crossed, according to what you learnt at the driving school or as a result of fines and suspensions of driving licence. This is a detail of minor importance for the Lebanese driver, always burning with impatience and eager to use the horn. He passes the other car when he thinks he can or when he is tired of waiting. And if he finds himself facing another vehicle head-on, fate must resolve the matter if it cannot be done by a flourish of the steering-wheel or a touch on the brake or accelerator. It usually is.

Moreover, it would appear that the speed of a vehicle is in direct proportion to its weight. A heavy truck is driven with the foot hard down. But even the most flagrant faults do not raise any protests on the part of the driver who might have been

Deir el-Qamar Mosk (Photo NCT - Yetenegian.)

the victim. He keeps quite calm, for he knows well enough that he might very well have done the same himself. At first, the visitor will be literally terrified by the mad risks taken by his driver on the hairpin bends of mountain roads. But he will soon realize that nobody can match the Lebanese driver for skill and, once he has got over his first frights, will consider motoring in Lebanon as a sort of joke carried a bit too far which he will look back on with indulgent amusement.

Creators or imitators?

Lebanese intelligence has often been accused of being down-to-earth and utilitarian because, from the time of the Phoenicians, business acumen and the esteem in which purely material success is held have always been the dominating features of the personality of the people. A rather unjustified accusation if we consider that this was the people who invented the phonetic alphabet of twenty-two letters — a supreme masterpiece of the power of abstract thought with which nothing throughout the history of mankind can be compared. The same critics consider that the Phoenicians and their descendants have never distinguished themselves by original works and have been little more than excellent imitators and followers. This is highly contestable.

Apart from the invention of the alphabet, an original step if ever there was one, and the art of navigation by reference to the Pole Star, what about the creation of Stoicism, the philosophical system of Zeno (333 to 261 BC), a Phoenician born in Cyprus, the works of Marinus of Tyre (first and second centuries AD), the inventor of mathematical geography who drew the first maps incorporating latitudes and longitudes, which formed the basis of those of Ptolemy, the work of Papinian and Ulpian, the great jurists of the Beirut Law School in the third century AD, that of the great pleiad of theologists formed by that same Law School, including Gregory of Nazianz, and that of modern Lebanese authors and scientists living in Lebanon or abroad, such as Georges Schéhadé and Khalil Gibran?

A religious people

Churches and mosques, Druze *khalwas*, a multitude of convents and monasteries perched on all high points and promontories, gigantic crosses illuminated at night, statues of the Virgin, innumerable altars with a light burning in them all along the roads of the Christian regions, church bells, the chant of the Muezzin, pilgrimages... Religion, or rather religions, are omni-present in Lebanon.

Places described by the name *mar* (holy), *deir* (convent) and *nabi* (prophet) are to be found everywhere. The Lebanese citizen describes himself by his membership of a religion, a sect or a rite. Officially, a Lebanese cannot be an atheist since he must be "on the books" of a religious authority. This, paradoxically enough, has resulted in a situation where this multi-confessional state has no official religion, which is unique in the Middle East. But that is far from indicating that Lebanon is a lay state.

Religion weighs heavily on the Lebanese spirit. Free thinkers are rare. Even those who profess a superficial atheism take their precautions in serious circumstances and conform to custom upon all solemn occasions.

The feast days

There are innumerable religious feast days to remind the Lebanese of his duties and allegiance and to maintain

*Except on feast days and festivals, the visitor rarely has the
chance to see traditional dress. A pity... but the beauty remains.
(Photo NCT.)*

Delicious fruit
which make one's mouth water,
in old Beirut's souks.

the fervour of the faithful. Some of these are local, but are no less striking for that, such as the feast of the Batroun fishermen on 16 August. A priest says Mass from a boat on the sea, surrounded by the boats of the fishermen, who meet afterwards to dance and feast. On 14 September the whole mountain is lit up for the feast of the Cross. There is a firework display, and fires are lighted on all the high points, on terraces and in church courtyards. Candles also burn on all terraces and balconies.

The feast of Saint Elias is the occasion for all sorts of rejoicings. There are fireworks. The bells sound out loud and young men from the villages vie with one another in their skill and strength in pulling the ropes.

There is a gloomy feast at Nabatiye in southern Lebanon which attracts enormous crowds. This is the "Achura", the commemoration by the Shiites of the brutal murder of the sons of Ali — Hassan and Hussein. The thousands of spectators (the figure of 50,000 is sometimes mentioned) are not all Shiites. They come to see the votaries of the Prophet's son-in-law re-live spectacularly the sufferings of the two martyrs. On a vast stage set up in the market square of this unattractive small town, men beat themselves with chains and strike themselves violently with the flats of knives. Their bodies are covered with blood. Women scratch their own faces, and a chorus of lamentations, shouts, groans and prayers arises. Each of those taking part drinks a mouthful of water from a jug and pronounces the usual phrase when speaking of someone who is no more: "Allah, yerhamu!" (May the Lord have pity on him!). But a little further on, the joys of the flesh take over. The cooks are cutting up the meat in preparation for the *kebbe* which they will sell to the spectators.

A wealth of legendary places

The Lebanese are imbued with religious feeling and so fond of legends that they are prepared to annex them if they can. It was at Nabi Younes, 33 km south of Beirut, that Jonah was disgorged by the whale. They show you his grave there. In the same way they show you the tomb of Noah near Zahle. But many other places and countries lay claim to the same honour.

Saint George slew the dragon at Beirut. Lebanon contains the tomb of Jacob at Niha (Nabi Yacoub). Elias ascended to heaven in his chariot of fire not far from Batroun, say the inhabitants as they invite the visitor to look at the spot from which he flew.

Lebanon had already been surfeited by antiquity. Europa, a Tyrian princess, was raped on the beach of Tyre by Zeus. Adonis was a child of Lebanon, and the coffin of Osiris was driven ashore at Byblos.

The Mosaic of religions

The mountain refuge and the persistence of outdated religious strife among groups of people permanently cut off from the world — a persistence due to a feeling of solidarity in the face of oppression — go a long way to explain the very odd religious and demographic structure of Lebanon and thus the particular features of its political institutions.

The Constitution recognizes seventeen different religions. The Lebanese Moslem can be a Sunnite, a Shiite or a Metuali; the Druze is a Jumblati or a Yasbaki; the Christian a Maronite, Orthodox, Greek Catholic, Syrian Catholic, Armenian Orthodox, Armenian Catholic, Chaldean, Protestant, etc... These communities, which were formerly kept in strictly watertight compartments were governed by different authorities. Nineteenth century travellers talk of a Moslem nation, a Maronite nation, a Druze

The wild valleys of northern Lebanon, such as that of the
Kadicha, were the refuge of the Maronites, who built churches
and monasteries there.
(Photo Almasy.)

nation, and so on. And yet today they have all been merged into the Lebanese nation.

The Maronites

The Maronites constitute one of the most numerous of the Lebanese communities. The history of these Christians, who appeared only in Lebanon, is full of vicissitudes. Saint Maron, the founder of the Maronite Church, pursued, in the region of Antioch, such an ascetic and exemplary life that, after his death in 423, his disciples erected a convent to contain his tomb and formed a separate community which spread rapidly. These Maronites, to escape from the persecution of the Byzantine emperors, moved up the valley of the Orontes and then, at the time of the Arab conquest, sought refuge in north Lebanon and took up fortified positions in the valley of the Kadisha, rejecting assimilation. From there, they spread throughout Mount Lebanon.

Today, they are particularly numerous in the Kesrouan. In the Metn and the Chouf, they lived peacefully side by side with the Druzes until the troubles of the nineteenth century which resulted in the events of 1860. The early years of the Maronite church when all sorts of heresies were flourishing and there were quarrels about the nature of Christ, were obscure, but the Maronites assert that they have never ceased to be faithful to Rome. Although Roman Catholics, their patriarch is known as the "Patriarch of Antioch and all the Orient". Their priests are allowed to marry.

The Druzes

Little is known about the Druzes — a fact related to the very doctrine of this sect which arose from a schism within Islam during the eleventh century. However, it is difficult to classify the Druzes as Moslems. They are not bound by the five obligations of Islam and the Koran is not their sacred book, although they do recite verses from it on special occasions. They have six sacred — and secret — books, including books written by the theorist to whom they owe their name — the Persian Darrazi — and collections of the sayings of Hakim, the Fatimide prophet of Cairo and first incarnation of their God. After the death of Darrazi, Hamzé, one of Hakim's disciples, in order to avoid further dissension, issued the edict: *"The curtain is drawn, the door closed, the ink dry and the pen broken."* These words and the Druzes' reticence concerning their doctrine (only the "*okals*", the wise men, have access to the "books") have shrouded Druzism in a deep mystery which makes an odd contrast with the apparent openness and simplicity of their behaviour. Lady Stanhope, that fanatical, eccentric Englishwoman who played a highly conspicuous part in Lebanese politics during the nineteenth century (her meeting with Lamartine, which the poet relates in his "Voyage en Orient", is a masterpiece of comedy), was passionately interested in the Druzes.

Druze doctrine is more of a moral than a metaphysical character. The *okals* have to lead a life of abstinence and poverty, and provide for themselves. The religion has no rites, but prayer and meditation. The Druzes assemble on Fridays in the "*khalwa*", a small house indistinguishable from any other. Like the Moslems, they have only one feast day — the "*Al-Adha*" — which celebrates Abraham's sacrifice. The Druzes believe in metempsychosis. "Le revenant," a novel by Khalil Takieddine, a former Lebanese ambassador, is founded on this belief. The

The cedars of Lebanon
are austere mountain-dwellers.

Near Deir el—Qamar, which was Fakhreddine's capital, Bechir the Great built the superb palace of Beit ed-Dine, the Lebanese beauty of which seems to recall the luxury of the past. (Photo NCT.)

objective of the *okal* is to attain the sublime state by purifying himself through successive lives, "just as metal goes through the test of fire". This belief explains the legendary courage of the Druzes and their disdain for death. Their moral code reveals itself in a marked sense of hospitality and honour and a profound attachment to the soil.

There are many Druzes in the centre of Mount Lebanon, in the Metn and the Chouf. In the village of Hasbaya and the neighbouring district, in the Wadi el-Taym where they first settled in Lebanon, they are in the majority. Syria contains as many Druzes as does Lebanon.

Confessionalism

The Lebanese religious communities have always played a decisive part in the political life of Lebanon. So great is their cohesion that their greatest fear is that of losing the special rights and advantages they have retained or acquired.

The Lebanese have learnt to live together. They even have great national pride. Nevertheless in everyday life, not very agreeable comments are sometimes made by the members of one community about those belonging to another. For example, none of the twelve to fifteen Christian communities is very indulgent towards its neighbours. Rivalry, intrigue and manoeuvring are rife. However, under the pressure of modern social ethics, the barriers between communities are beginning to fall. One of the most revealing and encouraging signs of this trend is the increase in the number of mixed marriages. Formerly, this practice could result in exclusion from the community. Those times are almost past, and young people are gradually shaking off the excessively limithing bonds of the community. In his book "Le peuple Libanais", Jean Salem tells that, "according to a survey carried out by a Lebanese weekly paper, 47 % of young men and women are in favour of the institution of civil marriage".

Lebanese institutions

Lebanese institutions are founded on the confession. The Constitution of 26 May 1926 states: "As a temporary measure and in the interests of justice and peace, the communities will be equitably represented in public employment and in the composition of the Cabinet". The electoral law provides for the proportional representation of the communities in Parliament. The latter consists of 99 representatives: 30 Maronites, 20 Sunnites, 19 Shiites, 11 Greek Orthodox, 6 Greek Catholics, 6 Druzes, 4 Armenian Orthodox, 1 Armenian Catholic, 1 Protestant and 1 Representative of the other minorities. But these representatives are elected by universal suffrage for a period of four years by all the electors of their constituencies, and not merely by their co-religionists.

This structure, which conforms to the confessions, is, however, counterbalanced by a strong central authority. In addition to the written Constitution, there is a tradition which has never hitherto been broken and which was ratified in the "National Pact" of 1943 signed by the "Resistance Government" formed in the mountain by Christians, Moslems and Druzes. This Pact instituted the Community Charter, according to which the President of the Republic is a Maronite, the Prime Minister a Sunnite, the Speaker a Shiite, and the Deputy Prime Minister a Greek Orthodox. Exactly the same proportions apply to the composition of the Cabinet. The President of the Repu-

A large number of churches, such as St John of Jbail whose curious baptistry is seen here, built at the time of the Crusades, bear witness to the religious fervour of the Lebanese. (Photo Almasy.)

blic, who holds office for six years and is elected by Parliament, thus represents a sort of multi-confessional concensus, which makes him a very powerful person. Thus, although the Cabinet is responsible to Parliament, the part played by the political parties (of which there are about a dozen) is very slight. What count in the political life of Lebanon are the communities and clans.

Feudalism

The survivals of a real feudal system dating back to the Emirs of Lebanon are still sometimes visible. This is a further complication of the Lebanese political situation — a veritable Chinese puzzle for the foreign observer accustomed to base the political geography of a country on parties.

Dispersion of the Lebanese people

The number of Lebanese living outside the country is not far from the number living in it. Some even claim that the number of emigrants is double population of Lebanon. No real statistics are available. The figures advanced vary from one to five million.

Emigration is a constant factor in Lebanese demography; it is bound up with the spirit of enterprise and love of travelling which used to characterize the Phoenicians. It is a big temptation to go off and seek a fortune in a distant country when your own offers only limited resources, and it is a temptation to which the dramatic events which occurred in the Lebanese mountain during the nineteenth century gave a vigorous fillip. The Lebanese Christians fled from Ottoman oppression to greater freedom and greater prosperity. The struggle between Druzes and Christians were at the origin of a major movement of emigration.

"Between 1860 and 1900," states Jean Salem in "Le Peuple libanais", "nearly 3,000 left every year; the movement speeded up between 1900 and 1914, and the annual figure rose to 15,000, falling again to 3,000 after the first World War. This also is the present figure. The slowing down of the movement as from 1920 can be at least partly explained by the creation of the Lebanese State, which put an end to Ottoman oppression.

"Today, more than 1,100,000 people of Lebanese origin are spread through the five continents. By far the most numerous groups are in the United States of America (400,000), Brazil (350,000), Argentina (150,000), and the countries of Black Africa. For some years, the main trend of Lebanese emigration has been towards Australia and Canada".

Lebanese emigrants, in general, are very attached to their country of origin even when they are assimilated to their country of adoption (and the Lebanese have a great capacity for assimilation). They like to go back there, dream of finishing their lives there, build houses there and frequently make gifts to their community... They also take a keen interest in Lebanese politics and, owing to their economic power (many have amassed vast fortunes) influence the country's future. Financial contributions by emigrants constitute a considerable share of the credit side of the Lebanese balance of payments. They also add to the intellectual status of the country, since a fair number of Lebanese have become famous abroad in the Arts, Sciences and Letters.

At Byblos, the past which is always assailing you goes back
without a break to the most ancient times.
(Photo Marinier.)

the painful birth of a nation

rom phoenicia to lebanon

*These statuettes of bronze covered with gold leaf are one
of the finest examples of Phoenician art (ex-voto of the
Hittite epoch) (Beirut National Museum).
(Photo NCT - Fulvio Roiter.)*

Old people - young nation

The road which this old people had to follow in order to succeed in forming a nation was a long and hard one. Today, as a space on the map, forged by community struggles against successive invaders in which internal rivalries disappeared, and confirmed in its validity, the Lebanese nation exists.

But the beginnings of its birth scarcely go back any further than the end of the sixteenth century. It was only slowly, very slowly, that the human groups composing it achieved that willingness to live together which is at the basis of any nation. And after all, there are few nations, even among the most powerful, which are not from time to time torn by internecine strife. Even if the Lebanese State is a young one, historically, it is not much younger than Germany, Italy and the United States.

Origins

Very little is known of the natives who lived in Lebanon in the pre-historical era. The region enters into history with the arrival of Semitic peoples from the steppes of Syria and Transjordania; the Canaanites, of whom one group formed the Phoenicians, came first during the third millenium B.C., and then the Amorites around 2150. But further invaders swept down on Mount Lebanon and the coast (see " the Lebanese nation and people").
"Trusting in the power of my lords Nebu and Marduk, I organized my army for an expedition to the Lebanon. I made that country happy by eradicating its enemy everywhere... I cut through steep mountains, I split rocks, opened passages and thus I connected a straight road for the transport of the cedars... In order that nobody might do any harm to the inhabitants of the Lebanon I erected there a stele showing me as everlasting king of this region.'' This is how the archaeologists deciphered the inscription of Nebuchadnezzar at Hermel (see note on this name).

Lebanon has known many liberators like Nebuchadnezzar, who said they were concerned about conferring happiness and prosperity on the countries they invaded. In reality, these kindly souls were motivated by imperialist interest alone. Protectors of this region in antiquity were innumerable. Nebuchadnezzar was only the first, and Babylon's "eternal" reign over Lebanon lasted only fifty-eight years. Others lasted for centuries. Egypt, which was alternately allied with and "protecting" the country, stayed there from the pre-dynastic epoch to 1720 B.C., when they were seen off by the Hyksos. They came back from the sixteenth to the fourteenth centuries The Hittites replaced them. Ramses II reconquered it from them and, for this mighty deed, engraved the first inscription on the Nahr al-Kalb.

The Phoenicians

At the beginning of the thirteenth century B.C., with the the disappearance of Egyptian and Hittite power and the rise of Assyria, the city-states of Phoenicia attained full independence, though Phoenicia was never politically united. The economic and trading interests of the towns composing it (Tyre, Sidon, Beryte, Bothrys, and Aradus) were divergent. Each of them had its tutelar divinity and king or oligarchy, a council of wise men formed of merchant aristocrats, rich sea-captains, and influential, respected citizens. Even so, at certain times these rival cities formed federations, headed by different towns: Ugarit in the sixteenth century, Gebla and Aradus in the fourteenth, Sidon in the twelfth, Tyre from the eleventh to the ninth, and Tripoli in the fifth century B.C. The Phoenicians extended their trading activities and established trading-posts and colonies all round the Mediterranean. They were to achieve unequalled fame as navigators and traders.

In Phoenicia itself their prosperous cities developed art and industry. They invented the alphabet, made glass almost as early as the Egyptians, and perfected the manufacture of purple, the most famous and sought after dye of antiquity. The perfection of the fabrics, embroideries, pottery, and copper, bronze, and silver vases produced by their artisans was known throughout the Mediterranean. Their art, initially inspired by Egyptian and Aegean techniques, became a model for archaic Greek art until the fifth century B.C.

But the basis of their economy was agriculture, fishing and trade. The Phoenicians kept sheep and cultivated cotton which had been introduced from India. It was they who introduced cotton fabrics into Greece. Great shipbuilders and capable navigators, they remained for a long time the rulers of the sea.

The Phoenician colonies (Carthage, the most famous, became a rival of Rome) were spread throughout the Mediterranean and even went beyond the Pillars of Hercules (Gades, the future Cadiz, was founded by the Phoenicians about 1000 B.C.). The navigators of Tyre and Sidon may have gone as far as Cornwall. In the sixth century B.C., Hanno sailed along the African coast as far as Fernando Po.

In spite of the Assyrian and Babylonian invasions, the prosperity of the Phoenicians and their maritime

THE PHOENICIAN RELIGION

The religion of the Phoenicians had very close affinity with that of the Chaldeans: they worshipped the forces of nature, the sun, the heavenly bodies personified divinities. Baal, which means Lord, was the generic title for the Gods; Baalat, which means Mistress, or Astarte, was that of the Goddesses, their wives. There was therefore a great number of Baals and of Astartes: each tribe, each town had its own. Thus, Melkart was the Baal of Tyre. The most important bore the title of Moloch (king) of the Gods.

The cult of the Phoenician Gods, following other pagan rites, was sanguinary. They required human victims and, at the time of great calamities, it was thought that the only way to appease the Gods was to sacrifice children to them, their parents being obliged to throw them alive into the sacred fire of the idols. The feasts of Adonis, God of Spring, who each year dies and resuscitates, were celebrated at Byblos with indescribable orgies. At Tyre, in order to appease the wrath of the Gods, it was customary for the kings to immolate their own sons. Individuals would do the same when they wished to divert some great misfortune that menaced them, or which dogged them. Those who did not have children of their own, and who did not wish to be deprived of the merit of such sacrifice, bought the children of poor people.

Antoine Sfeir
"Liban", 4/3/1973

supremacy only really began to decline in favour of the Greeks after Alexander's conquest (333 B.C.). Even so, after the establishment of the *Pax Romana* with the Roman conquest of 64 B.C., Phoenicia, which then consisted of the coast, Mount Lebanon and the Bekaa, once again became relatively prosperous, as is witnessed by the amazing complex of Baalbek and the innumerable Roman temples. It disappeared, however, in the seventh century.

Christian Lebanon

Not far from the Holy Places, Lebanon was one of the first regions to become Christian. Saint Paul crossed the country twice. At the end of the second century, Tyre was a bishopric. A synod was held there in 335. There were many Christians at the Beryte Law School, and Lebanon was proud of the number of martyrs as a result of the persecution of Diocletian (including St George). Soon, however, the first Christian Emperor, Constantine, and his mother, Helen, ordered the destruction of the pagan temples. Christianity became the official religion of Syria, Lebanon and Palestine. Meanwhile, the splitting of the Roman Empire into Western and Eastern Empires placed Lebanon under the authority of Byzantium, which showed itself to be much less liberal than Rome.

The inhabitants of the former Phoenicia, crippled with taxes, closed their ranks, refused to speak Greek or Latin, and retained their own language — Aramaean (or Syriac) — the use of which as a form of resistance to foreign domination and an assertion of the people's personality, continued for centuries more. Authoritarian Byzantine rule resulted in the proliferation of Christian heresies (Nestorianism, Monophysism, Monothelism) all of which were concerned with the

*Baalbek, symbolical of Roman power in Asia, with its grandiose
ruins in the heart of the Bekaa.
(Photo Almasy.)*

mystery of incarnation and the nature of Christ. Discussion raged in the Lebanese mountain, and these theological disputes are at the origin of the proliferation of Christian churches in Lebanon today.

Lebanon and Islam

After the battle of Yarmouk in 636, the Arabs invaded Lebanon under the banner of Islam; the sea terrified these new conquerors from the desert.They did not immediately occupy the coast, but the famous Caliph Moawia, who founded the Ommiad dynasty in Damascus, did not hesitate to exploit the talents of the navigators and shipbuilders who had descended from the Phoenicians to build a fleet in order to be able to counter any possible return of the Byzantines. The inhabitants of the region, weary of Byzantine domination, cooperated all the more easily with the newcomers owing to the fact that the Moslem yoke was light. Neither Moawia nor his successors persecuted the Christians, who even provided senior administrators to the first Caliph of Bagdad.

It was only with the coming of the Abbassides (750) that the situation deteriorated and that most of the Christian Arabs were forced to embrace Islam. The mountain-dwellers revolted and had a few initial successes, but were finally defeated near Baalbek, taken from their villages and dispersed in Syria. But Arab power was shaken on two occasions, once by a Byzantine invasion in the tenth century and once by an invasion from the Seljuks who occupied Syria, at the beginning of the eleventh century.

The Lebanese coast relapsed into anarchy. The Arab Empire was divided between the Abbasside dynasty in Bagdad and the Fatimide dynasty in Cairo, and Islam was torn

The temple of Bacchus — the best preserved of the Baalbek temples.
(Photo Almasy.)

Anjar, a caravanserai of Arab princes, destroyed at the time of the
Ommiads, rises in defiance of the centuries at the edge of the
Anti-Lebanon.
(Photo NCT.)

between the two rival sects. The orthodox Moslems persecuted the heretics, who took refuge in the mountains, ready to applaud the victories over their rivals which the Mongols and the Franks were to score later. Thus, the latter found in the mountains support among the persecuted peoples.

Lebanon and the Crusaders

The Crusades, which placed the Near East under Frankish domination for two centuries, caused more suffering to Lebanon than to any other region. The Mamelukes, that dynasty of former slaves which replaced the Fatimides in the thirteenth century, practised a burnt-earth policy for the purpose of reprisals. In addition to this, the unfortunate country suffered earthquakes and Mongolian invasions. "I journeyed to the fort of Askalon," wrote Ibn-Battutah in his diary in 1326, "now a heap of ruins... Then I arrived in Akka, once capital of the Franks in Syria but now a ruin... Then I journeyed to Tyre, which is a ruin with a populous village outside of it".

Philip K. Hitti, in "A Short History of Lebanon", tells us of the experience of Sidon during and after the Crusades: "in 1107 Sidon purchased an uncertain immunity from a threatened siege; in 1111 it was captured by Baldwin I, 1187 dismantled by Salah-al-Din, 1197 recovered by Crusaders, in the same year regained and destroyed by Moslems, rebuilt by Franks 1228, redevastated by Moslems 1249, restored and refortified by Louis IX 1253, ravaged by Mongols 1260, regained by al-Ashraf in 1291 and razed to the ground. No wonder modern times found this city a miserable caricature of its former self."

The Maronites, who had welcomed the Crusaders warmly, provided them

*The vast excavation site of Tyre opens onto the sea in the
midst of rose-laurels.
(Photo Marinier.)*

with guides and sent their skilled archers to fight alongside the Franks, were hard hit by the repression. The Mamelukes penetrated into Kadisha and destroyed Becharre, Ehden and Hadeth ej-Jobbe. Equally severe measures were taken against the schismatic Moslems, Shiites and Druzes. These persecutions brought together the mountaineers who had suffered from them. An embryo of national consciousness began to emerge from misfortune.

But the Crusaders — that highly suspect pillaging foray and exercise in economic conquest under the guise of religious proselytism and protection of the Holy Places — resulted, paradoxically, in a rapprochement between East and West, who began to know and understand each other better. The fact is that the periods of peace were much longer than the periods of war. After the departure of the Crusaders, in spite of frequent incursions by the Franks, commercial and cultural relations, as a result of which the West learnt a great deal from the East, increased continually. And Lebanon was destined to be the privileged centre for these new relations.

Fakhreddin

This is the first great Lebanese statesman we know about. Out of the multitude of Emirs who reigned over their individual piece of mountain, squabbled and fought with each other, and whose authority was tolerated by the Turks, who dominated the region from 1516 onwards, there was to emerge, at the end of the sixteenth century, the first unifier of Lebanon, Fakhreddin II, Emir of the Druzes, of the Maan family. This little man (''an egg falling from his pocket wouldn't break,'' said his enemies), this intelligent and cunning Emir of the Chouf eliminated his most powerful neighbouring Emirs one after the other, and extended his authority to the whole of north Lebanon, and the

The Emir Amine, son of Bechir II, built an elegant palace
which towers over that of Beit ed-Dine.
(Photo NCT.)

Bekaa then to south Lebanon and to Galilee.

His apparent submission to the Porte (he paid his tribute regularly) and the Sultan's troubles elsewhere ensured that he remained immune for a long time. Fakhreddin forged close links with fore·gn countries, negotiated with the Grand Duke of Tuscany like an independent sovereign, and developed his commerce and industry. Pride, however, was due for a fall. The Pasha of Damascus aroused the less docile vassals against him, invaded Lebanon and sacked it. Fakhreddin went into exile, in Italy, where he remained for five years. He returned in 1618 and reigned a further seventeen years to his greater glory. When, in 1634, the Turks decided to stake everything on overthrowing him, he "had attained such a degree of power that all he had to do was to claim the Sultanate," as the historian Mohibbi says. Beaten, Fakhreddin took refuge in the caves of Niha (see note on Jezzine), but the Turks poisoned his water supply, and he was forced to come out. He surrendered to the Turks, who executed him on 13 April 1635.

Fakhreddin, a tolerant Emir whose palaces at Deir al-Qamar recall his grandeur, was a great builder and brought prosperity and unity to Lebanon. He set up the first printing presses in the Levant, undertook extensive irrigation works and planted a fine pine forest near Beirut. In foreign politics, he always favoured a rapprochement with the West, particularly Italy and France, thereby indicating a specifically Lebanese characteristic. He suppressed all religious discrimination, and thus can be considered the real founder of modern Lebanon.

Bechir the Great

After the fall of Fakhreddin, Lebanon returned to its internal strife, but the experience of that Emir was never to be forgotten. Power passed to the hands of the Chehab family, related to

*The palace of Beit ed-Dine, summer residence of the President
of the Lebanese Republic, also contains a folk-lore museum.
(Photo Almasy.)*

*From "Château des Croisés" in Byblos, one's sight runs
easily from the ruins and the sea.*

Tripoli…
(Photo M. Guillard.)

the Maans, and another Emir, Bechir II (1788 to 1840), whose memory is perpetuated in the magnificent palace of Beit ed-Dine, was again to unite Lebanon under the sign of tolerance, such tolerance that the Emir himself simultaneously adopted three religions. The result was that when, after independence, his ashes were brought back to Lebanon, this gave rise to three religious ceremonies: one Moslem, one Christian, one Druze.

A fierce warrior, Bechir II also extended his power far and wide, almost independently of Constantinople. He never hesitated to use pitiless force to maintain order in the Lebanese mountain.

He, too, had to go into exile, but he had bound up his destiny with that of Mehemet-Ali, the Viceroy of Egypt. The latter, at first victorious in his fight against the Sultan, finally had to put an end to the occupation of the Ottoman provinces, faced with the intervention of the European powers, not including France. The Egyptians, as a result of their financial exactions, had aroused the hatred of the oppressed Lebanese. Bechir was forced to abdicate by an insurrection of his subjects of all confessions.

At Antelias, on 8 June 1860, the twelve members of a committee representing the various communities swore brotherhood on the altar of the Maronite sanctuary of Saint Elias and demanded the setting up of a council of communities. For the first time, the different communities expressed their solidarity and their will to live together in a country wich was taking its destiny into its own hands. This solidarity, asserted against Bechir, was however the result of his policy of religious peace and understanding among the various communities.

Druzes versus Maronites

In his intransigence, Bechir, in order to maintain Lebanese unity and provide support for Mehemet-Ali, had had to attack the Druzes who opposed the Egyptian occupation. He had even used certain Maronites for this repression. Religious strife sprang up again after the Emir's abdication, and this was aggravated by feudal struggles during which members of the various communities fought on both sides. Stirred up from outside by Turkey and England (which was concerned at the Maronites'pro-French attitude), this internal struggle was transformed into a series of veritable civil wars.

The Turkish solution to the problem — eviction of the Chehabs and a return to direct administration with an artificial division into two "Caimacamats" (Maronites to the north of the Beirut-Damascus road and Druzes to the south) only made matters worse. It resulted in a tragic confrontation between Christians and Druzes under the indifferent or conniving eyes of the Turks.

Peace was restored by the intervention of foreign powers (a French expeditionary force landed at Beirut in September 1860) and tardy but energetic action on the part of the Turks. The European powers then insisted that the Porte should set up an autonomous "mustassarifat" (administration) of Lebanon. This was only a tiny Lebanon including neither the Wadi-Taym, the seat of the Chehab family, nor the Bekaa, nor Beirut, nor Saida. Nevertheless, this small Lebanon lived in peace until the first World War.

Independence

On 1 September 1920, General Gouraud, representing France which was to become a mandatory power, officially proclaimed the independence of "Greater Lebanon" with frontiers as they are at present. The Constitution of 26 May 1926 substituted the title "Lebanese Republic'' for "Greater Lebanon". But Lebanon still had to fight to wrest its complete independence from France. After the battles between the French Troops of the Levant (controlled by the Vichy Government) and the Anglo-Australian army in 1941, the French attempted to maintain a control over Lebanon which was rejected by the Lebanese population. As a result of the 1943 elections, a nationalist majority emerged, which elected Bechara al-Khury as President of the Republic. He and the Prime Minister, Riad Solh, utterly rejected French control. The Delegate General of Free France had them arrested and imprisoned in the fortress of Rachaya. A "Resistance Government" was then formed in the mountain. Its members, belonging to all communities, proclaimed the famous "National Pact", the provisions of which constitute the basis of present-day Lebanese institutions. General de Gaulle dispatched General Catroux with all speed, to free the prisoners and restore peace. The independence of Lebanon was recognized without any restrictions and the last French troops were withdrawn in 1946.

In spite of a few serious crises, Lebanon has since been less disturbed than other Middle East countries. This is an argument in favour of the country's institutions.

THE ADMINISTRATION OF LEBANON

For the purpose of administration, the Lebanese Republic is divided into five regional governments (moafazat):—
■ Beirut
■ North Lebanon, subdivided into six cazas — Akkar, Tripoli, Zghorta, Becharre, Koura, Batroun.
■ Mount Lebanon, subdivided into five cazas — Jbail, Kesrouan, Baabda, Aley, Chouf.
■ South Lebanon, subdivided into seven cazas — Saida, Jezzine, Nabatiye, Marjayoun, Hasbaya, Sour, Bent Jbail.
■ The Bekaa, subdivided into five cazas — Western Bekaa, Rachaya, Zahle, Baalbek, Hermel.
Each regional government is headed by a moafez appointed by the Government, and each caza is headed by a caimacam also appointed by the Government.
Boroughs are administered by municipal councillors who elect their mayor.

lebanon today and tomorrow

The "Borj" (Place des Martyrs or Place des Canons), the ancient centre of the town of Beirut, is still teeming with life today. (Photo M. Guillard.)

"The only happiness possible will be that of detachment... the only wealth that of watching the summer follow spring and the wistaria flowering and the storks flying and the play of light..." The author of these words was a great Lebanese political theorist, Michel Chiha (1891 to 1954). This wisdom, this peace and this poetry belong to the eternal mountain. Their distant image imbues with nostalgia the pitiless activity of the city-dweller and provides an alibi for the fierceness of commercial competition. There is nothing less detached than Lebanon today.

A baffling economy

A curious country, situated in an under-developed region and from certain points of view having the structure of a country in process of development, but with economic statistics equivalent to those of the most highly developed countries. Gross national product per head of the population must have attained 800 dollars in 1972, which is by no means negligible.

Even for the visitor who does not trouble to take more than a superficial look, one thing is obvious — while Lebanon is a country where the most insolent luxury exists side by side with a certain degree of poverty, poverty in its most cruel form is absolutely non-existent. There are no beggars or wretched children with pot-bellies. The most indigent mountain children radiate health. And nearly everywhere we find that luxury obtained at the cost of who knows what sacrifices among the poor — cleanliness. The Lebanese are clean and their country smells good.

As for the wealth displayed with so much ostentation, its origin would appear to be enigmatic, for this country, where a considerable minority live in luxury and whose currency is one of the hardest in the world, produces practically nothing. Lebanon was not lucky enough to find oil under the soil, like its neighbours, nor any other mineral deposits. Its only natural wealth is the fertility of part of the soil.

Agriculture - the traditional resource

Agriculture certainly is the traditional resource of this country of orchards and livestock. The climate and relief of Lebanon make it possible to produce a very wide range of the fruits which are in demand; both those of hot countries and temperate countries — apples, oranges, lemons, mandarines, grapefruit, bananas, grapes, pears, peaches, plums, apricots, cherries, pomegranates, etc... Citrus fruits are at the head of the list, followed closely by apples. As for livestock, this consists essentially of mountain goats and Bekaa sheep. Poultry - keeping is the only agricultural sector which is expanding. Exports of fruit 333,551 tons in 1972, including 137,282 tons of apples) account for a considerable share of Lebanese foreign trade, 90 % going to Arab countries.

But today, as Riad F. Saadé wrote in the 1973 special issue of "Le Commerce du Levant", "agriculture could have been the chief wealth of Lebanon and one of the best sources of revenue, in view of the favourable natural conditions as compared with those generally prevailing in the region — climate, hydrography, variety of soil, numerous labour force, etc. It is not, because man takes very little interest in helping nature... For the past thirty years, Lebanese agriculture has been declining in favour of other sectors which are more lucrative and less subject to risks. Since then, the share of the national revenue accounted for by agriculture started to decrease until, in 1972, it accounted for less than 10 % of it."

The Bekaa, the fertile plain which stretches between the Lebanon and the Anti-Lebanon, contains the richest land in the country.
(Photo M. Guillard.)

Lebanese industry

Although bereft of raw materials other than foodstuffs, Lebanon has made a great industrialization effort since independence. Today, it is trying to find markets for a production which is in excess of domestic requirements, "Apart from a very limited number of factories, Lebanese firms are operating, for the most part, at less than two thirds of their production potential owing to lack of markets," writes Nabil Ladki, General Secretary of the Association of Lebanese Manufacturers. Lebanese industrial production has made a vast stride forward during the past decade, and industrial investments increased from 587 million Lebanese pounds in 1960 to 1,300 million in 1971, while exports increased from 39 to 370 million over the same period.

But, as the visitor to Lebanon soon realizes, this industry is a very small one. Apart from the two big refineries at Beddawi and Zahrani and the Chekka cement-works, he sees few factories worthy of attention. Lebanese industry produces little except food products (fruit juice, biscuits, preserves and sugar), tobacco, cement, hydrocarbon, textile, footwear and leather goods. And even there, the products of craftsmen accounted for 24 % in 1964.

Balance of payments mysteries

As we know, Lebanon is a trading country which perpetuates a tradition going back to the Phoenicians. The Lebanese are traders. They live from trade. This is obvious even to the least attentive observer. Of course, there are individuals who make lots of money by broking. But normally, the country ought to go bankrupt, for its foreign trading balance shows a certain deficit.

Imports into Lebanon are enormous and exports few.

The mystery of this situation is only apparent. All kinds of more or less invisible earnings more than make up for the trading deficit — profits on triangular operations, transfers of funds from emigrants, entries of foreign capital, earnings from foreign investments, "royalties" from oil pipelines, clandestine trading in gold, and of course, the tourist industry. This country, which sells little and buys without counting the cost, has chosen to be one of the chief banking and taxation refuges in the world. This is what is known as the Lebanese "economic miracle".

A bankers'paradise

Lebanon is swamped with foreign capital. Here, banking secrecy in favour of the customer is the most complete in the world. Bank staffs are forbidden to reveal the names of customers or their balances not only to individuals but also to government or legal authorities. In addition, bank balances cannot be seized. This legislation dates from 1956.

In 1945, there were only seven large banks in Lebanon. Between 1945 and 1955, fifteen new ones were set up in Beirut, followed by eighteen more between 1955 and 1960. In 1964, the number of banks had reached ninety-three. The failure of the Intra Bank in 1966 and the Six-Day war in 1967 shook this magnificent banking edifice. A score of banks disappeared, but the survivors did not have to wait long for the good days to come again.

In December 1972, seventy-four banking establishments were operating in Lebanon, nineteen of which covered all the international banking houses. Over the same period, the amount of deposit increased at breakneck speed — 20 million Lebanese pounds in 1939, 200 million in 1947, 1,000 million in 1959, 4,000 million in 1970 and 5,800 million at the end of 1972.

*Wind-pumps, which irrigate the large salt marshes spread along
the coast between Tripoli and Batroun.
(Photo NCT - Fulvio Roiter.)*

Economic liberalism.

The prosperity of Lebanon is founded on absolute economic liberty. This policy explains the apparent inequality of incomes. But it gives a brilliant aspect of prosperity and fosters all commercial activity.

"Liberalism in trade," writes Pierre Nasrallah, General Secretary of the Association of Lebanese Banks, "confers a very special character on the commerce of the country — absence of all trading restrictions such as transfer permits, exchange authorizations, etc... Financial facilities offered in Beirut are, for a businessman, an attraction which taxation cannot affect. Traders can pay any supplier in any currency and thus carry out commercial operations with the greatest of ease. Economic liberalism facilitates commercial operations and particularly fosters triangular operations. The free exchange area of Beirut strengthens that centre in playing the part of pivot and intermediary."

Increasing activity at the port of Beirut and at the international airport of Khalde bears witness to this privileged situation. Traffic on this scale provides Lebanon with considerable revenue from customs charges, which increased from 146 million in 1967 to 305 million in 1972.

As far as its economic policy and conduct of business are concerned, Lebanon much resembles the United States; but its small area and the community structure, which is considered as a necessary evil and results in a political and economic conservatism which can also be described as stability, enable it to protect free enterprise much more effectively than even the most conservative governments of the great American Republic. Any attempt at state control is resented by the *beati possidentes* as an intolerable attack on liberty.

Intellectual activity

But business Lebanon is not the real Lebanon. There is also a Lebanon interested in intellectual matters, philosophy, art and literature, whose activity and production have always been remarkable. As a meeting place of civilizations, Lebanon receives impulses of various origins favouring the eruption of intense intellectual activity. As against the many influences which, in this field, make themselves felt and provide inspiration, the Lebanese personality has a certain difficulty in asserting itself. The fact that a considerable number of Lebanese are bilingual may partly explain this.

But thought and art today tend to move towards a sort of planetary unity as a result of a permanent osmosis between countries. Who could distinguish an American abstract painting from one done by a Frenchman, Italian, German or Englishman? Men differ, but nations increasingly resemble one another. Lebanon was a pioneer, open as it was to everything human and providing great writers in French and English as well as Arabic.

A scholastic tradition

The country where the alphabet was invented would be betraying its destiny if it lacked schools, and indeed Lebanon has a very high school attendance rate. 95 % of all boys and 89 % of all girls from six to nine years of age go to school; 89 % of all boys and 78 % of all girls are still at school from ten to fourteen years of age; 55 % of boys and 38 % of girls continue to the age of nineteen; and 26 % and 9 % respectively go to university.

In 1969, the State was running 874 primary schools and 410 secondary schools (including technical schools), but there are also a large number of private schools. In addition to those of each community there are those of the many teaching orders; these are often imposing buildings like large modern convents and, like them, perched high on magnificent sites. There are also a large number of foreign schools in this eminently tolerant country, where liberalism is an inviolable principle. There are four universities, only one of which is Lebanese (to which must be added the *Ecole supérieure des Lettres*, a faculty of Lyons University, and its centre for mathematical studies). The result is that the education required for the various university degrees is somewhat divergent and that there is a remarkable proportion of educated persons.

The degrees of the various universities vary widely in value.

A Press in four languages

What with its dozen political parties, the individualism of its citizens and their tendency to be polyglot, Lebanon could not fail to have a large number of widely varying newspapers. The Lebanese have a choice between forty-two political dailies. Two major Arabic newspapers, "Al-Nahar" and "Al-Anwar", have a circulation of 75,000. These are followed by "Al-Hayat", "Al-Moharrer" and "Al-Jaryda". There are three French-language dailies: "L'Orient-Le Jour", the biggest, "As-Safa", and "Le Soir". In addition, there are an English-language daily, "Daily-Star", and four Armenian dailies. There is also a wealth of weeklies.The Ministry of Information publishes the periodical "Lebanon", while the National Council for Tourism brings out a monthly bulletin in French and English, "Liban Gazette" ("Lebanon Gazette").

ONE EMBRACES THE WHOLE WORLD

Lebanon, which name covers the whole of the Kesrouan Chain and the country of the Druzes, offers the complete spectacle of the great mountains. One finds there at each step that scenery which nature deploys, now for its pleasant aspect or grandeur, later for its outlandishness, but always for its diversity. Should one approach by sea, or descend to the shore, the height and steepness of this rampart, which seems to enclose the earth, the gigantic mass of which pierces the sky inspires astonishment and respect. Should the curious observer climb to the summits which obstructed his view, the immensity of the space unfolded before him becomes one more subject for his amazement; but to be enabled to fully enjoy the majesty of the spectacle, he must climb to the summit of the Lebanon or the Sannine. There, in all directions, extends a horizon without limits. There, in clear weather, the view spreads out over the desert enclosing the Persian Gulf and the sea which bathes the shores of Europe. In imagination, one embraces the whole world.

VOLNEY
"Voyage en Egypte et en Syrie"

Culture and bilingualism

"I lived for a long time in the most beautiful country in the world", said Gabriel Bunure, a great poetry critic who was head of the Ecole Supérieure des Lettres in Beirut. He was speaking of Lebanon. The passionate love for Lebanon of this remarkably unfettered and sensitive intellect, with his flair for discovering talent, was certainly due to a large extent to his appreciation of the intellectual climate of the Lebanese capital. A climate, no doubt, excessively French and too "uprooting" for young writers and artists who had unhesitatingly chosen Paris as a model, but a climate bubbling with the effervescence which encourages creation.

The effervescence is still there. Lebanese cultural life has lost nothing of the intensity and vitality which formerly marked its Western, and particularly French, character and has since been extended to its Eastern and Arab aspect. The first could — and still can — be reproached for being somewhat vitiated, fundamentally, by worldliness and social or intellectual snobbery. The avant-garde Lebanese intellectual takes great care not to let himself be overtaken; he looks for what is rare and adores the coterie. But don't all avant-garde intellectuals? The society cocktail-party has other dangers. Some get caught up in them.

Though Western influences have left their mark, Lebanon was nevertheless a pioneer in the renaissance of Arab culture at the end of the nineteenth century. This duality is still today a distinctive characteristic of the intellectual life of Lebanon. This, of course, was partly the consequence of bilingualism. But apart from the use of two languages and the existence of two cultures, there is a danger in inconsiderate talk of acculturation. There is a certain specifically Lebanese character which attempts to express itself in both languages, sometimes pathetically. From the greatest works there emerges a singular poetry which, in its most profound expression, has a purely Lebanese resonance.

Writers in Arabic

An original Lebanese literature, escaping from pure exercise in rhetoric and compilation, began to assert itself half way through the ninenteenth century. This was the "*Nahda*", the renaissance of Arab letters, which was to spread throughout the entire Arab world, from Beirut to Cairo. Arab Lebanese literature today has shown itself worthy of its great ancestors. Poets, novelists and essayists of high quality are so numerous that a list of them would be monotonous, and a selection arbitrary. Unfortunately for the foreign reader, few have been systematically translated — a few works of the excellent poet Adonis (Ali Ahmed Said) and the novel "I live" by Layla Baalbaki are notable exceptions.

Lebanese writers in Arabic, both poets and novelists, very much resemble their French colleagues, many of whose works they have translated. They, too, want to change the face of poetry. Traditional novelists such as Marun Abbud and Khalil Takieddine have been followed by novelists of the absurd, despair and revolt.

Writers in French

The old school of Lebanese writers in French sang unceasingly of their native Lebanon, using the techniques of the Parnassians and the symbolists. Lebanon is a country of poets. Charles Corm (1894 to 1963), a fecund poet and playwright in the classical style and author of "La Montagne inspirée", founded in 1920 "La Revue Phénicienne", in which the Lebanese poets most renowned at that time —

*A fruit which poses a thorny problem to the non-initiated,
the prickly pear.
(Photo Marinier.)*

Michel Chiha, Elie Tyan, Hector Klat, etc., — expressed themselves in these same techniques.

The following generation had a more subtle ear and a more secret voice, and made more mysterious allusions. It had understood the lessons of Rimbaud and the surrealists. Two names are outstanding - Fuad Gabriel Naffah, a rare, strangely limpid poet and, above all, Georges Schéhadé; poetry makes the man. Schéhadé undertakes startling, serious games by means of which he transfigures reality, which has become transparent, into a series of images. Schéhadé's dramatic works are played in all the great theatres of the world. This internationally renowned writer has been translated into a score of languages.

There are many Lebanese writers of quality who express themselves in French. Apart from poets, there are novelists (the novel was scarcely known in Beirut before the last war) such as Farjallah Haik, and essayists such as René Habachi and Salah Stétié. Some of them, such as the excellent writer Andrée Chédid, live in France.

Lebanese emigrants, who found themselves freer than in their own country under Ottoman domination, became famous writers in their countries of adoption. By far the most famous is Khalil Gibran, author of the "Prophet", who wrote first in Arabic and then in English. On account of the extent of Lebanese emigration to Brazil, there are also Lebanese authors who write in Portuguese.

Theatre and cinema

There are six theatres for the 800,000 inhabitants of Beirut. Many amateur dramatic societies are beginning to merge in an original way with the professionals.

Plays are given in four languages - Arabic, French, English and Armenian. There is only a limited number of performances of each play. There would appear to be a shortage of authors. Even the Arab theatre mainly produces translations. But the Baalbek Festival has encouraged the more valid companies to go beyond the amateur stage. There is even a "Modern Theatre School", carrying on very up-to-date research, which gave an interesting performance at the International Theatre Festival at Deir el-Qamar in August and September 1973. The Lebanese cinema is beginning to find an audience outside the country.

The plastic arts

The recent independence of Lebanon has not allowed the creation of a tradition in plastic arts. Until recently, painters and sculptors inserted themselves more or less happily into the ways of the Paris School. Among the older ones, a painter such as Georges Cyr, who worked with Dufy and Matisse, was undoubtedly at the origin of a major revival of interest in the plastic arts. But it is above all the rapid increase in wealth of a part of Lebanese society which has opened up new future prospects to painters and caused an upheaval of ideas and the partial demolition of established reputations.

A new generation has arisen and launched an important movement which is more demanding in the search for its identity. Young painters certainly bring a new tone to painting without too many concessions to passing fashions. Things are less clear with the sculptors — the Basbus brothers, Salwa Rawda Chubair and Muazzaz Rawda.

The arts and letters in Lebanon, if they can avoid the pitfalls of mundanity and the emasculating coteries, are characterized by promising trends worthy of their great past and a receptive attitude to modernity.

Modern glassware and Phoenician pottery, the product of artisans whose craft goes back to very ancient times, are stil in fashion. (Photo M. Guillard.)

Folklore, colourful and original, has its place in the Baalbek Festival.
(Photo by the Office of the Baalbek International Festival.)

the lebanon of the poets

In the contented wonder of the
years
Amidst the splendour of snow and
verdure
With its seasons of four harvests
Eternal Lebanon is enthroned in the
sky
Each day, each night since thousands of years
It is the same giant bending towards
the sea
Who spinning the hours on his
fingers, counts each minute
At times tormented, more often
entranced
Enraged in winter, prancing in
summer
But never to the point of forgetting
the wager
Made the morning of Eve between
the archangel and himself
Covered by two words — Lebanon
and Deathless
Binding him to remain fierce and
on his guard
At the place where the two
conditions
Of joy and misfortune forebode
danger
But merely with weary mien he
gazes
Eyes and mirrors bent on the
horizon of the seas.

FOUAD GABRIEL NAFFAH
"La description de l'homme,
du cadre et de la lyre"

When the night is brilliantly
scattered
When thought is untouchable
I say mountain flower meaning
Solitude
I say liberty meaning despair
And as a woodman I take my steps
To mislead the lies
In a forest of trees
Full of justice and romance

GEORGES SCHÉHADÉ
"Poésies II"

A sunset
The God who moves in the heights
In the liberty of his elements
Having struck the sun with his cane
Very wise in the play of the snow
and the rain
The royal disc of clearness sounds
Tarnishes and falls into the swamp
Exciting the green skin of the frogs
And the black greediness of the
toads

FOUAD GABRIEL NAFFAH
"La description de l'homme,
du cadre et de la lyre"

Cedars, cedars of God, who will
say, who can tell
Your regal nobleness and your
majesty,
You who saw sink innumerable
empires
Under your eternity;
Question the skies whose eyes
admire you;
Pursue with God the enchanted
colloquy;
Play the plainsong on your giant
lyres,
Of our revolted hearts!

CHARLES CORM
"La montagne inspirée"

My brother, I have seen again the
    sky of our mountain;
And with my eyes which have so
    long wept for you,
I have seen again the most adored
    of countries.
I have seen again the green
    splendour of its countryside.
My brother, I have seen again its
    forests; I have seen again
Its fields, its streams, its ferns, its
    footpaths;
Unexhausted treasures, marvellous
    rebirths
Of which, alas! you are for ever
    deprived.
I have seen again each corner of the
    soil we loved
With such fervent love that in our
    common emotion
We felt more joined in our two
    souls.
I have seen all again, alas! I have
    seen all again... without you!

               HECTOR KLAT
         "Du cèdre au lys"

Improvised dialectic poetry, origi-
nating from Andalusia, sometimes
to be printed, the "Zajal" can still
be heard in Lebanon. Sometimes,
to the rhythm of a tambourine, the
professional choristers, invited on
important occasions, improvise for
engagement parties, weddings,
electoral rounds. Offensive,
counter-offensive, metaphors, as-
sonances, onomatopoeias, follow
one another in veritable rhymed
duels, a kind of complicity being
established between the artists and
the audience. The latter can
propose a theme and, even during
the course of an improvisation,
propose another theme to enliven
the joust. A popular poetry,
sometimes tender and transparent,
the "Zajal" flows forth without
affectation.
"... In the early morning
You and I will stroll amongst the
              lilies
With the butterflies".

         ANDRÉE CHÉDID
          "Liban",
       Petite Planète,
    (Editions du Seuil.)

And tell me, people of Orphalese,
what have you in these houses?
And what is it you guard with
fastened doors?
Have you peace, the quiet urge that
reveals your power?
Have you remembrances, the
glimmering arches that span the
summits of the mind?
Have you beauty, that leads the
heart from things fashioned of
wood and stone to the holy
mountain?
Tell me, have you these in your
houses?
Or have you only comfort, and the
lust for comfort, that stealthy thing
that enters the house a guest, and
then becomes a host, and then a
master?

Ay, and it becomes a tamer, and
with hook and scourge makes
puppets of your larger desires.
Though its hands are silken, its
heart is of iron.
It lulls you to sleep only to stand by
your bed and jeer at the dignity of
the flesh.
It makes mock of your sound
senses, and lays them in thistle-
down like fragile vessels.
Verily the lust for comfort murders
the passion of the soul, and then
walks grinning in the funeral.

           KHALIL GIBRAN
          "The Prophet"

town by town
from afqa to zouk mkayel

afqa

■ A gaping black opening on the side of a steep, rough, high cliff of a reddish colour. During the summer, two or three streams of water issuing from this dark mouth turn the rocks blue. But in spring this becomes a powerful jet, scarcely interrupted by the vault, which is invisible from below; it roars in fury, foams, and rushes down in a majestic sheet, bathes the greenery at the bottom of the valley in mist, and still growling as it goes beneath the bridge, passes over another fall and calms down in the huge pool at a lower level than the road.

The pool is so clear in summer that this cold "fountain" is an invitation to the narcissistic ritual of bathing — a lustral, ritual bath! For here we are in a sacred place, and even the "civilized" man of the twentieth century, whether consciously or subconsciously, cannot remain insensitive to the mystic power which has made it the scene of certain phantasms ever since man approached it for the first time.

The Adonis river

Afqa, the grotto of Adonis, is the source of the river Adonis of the Ancients — today the Nahr Ibrahim, which runs into the Mediterranean 6 kilometres south of Jbail (Byblos). The valley of the river is impressive on account of its savage grandeur and its tortured shapes. One can drive part of the way up it by means of a narrow, but asphalted, road which runs along the bottom of the valley for about 10 kilometres. At the start, where it is surrounded by reeds, there is a pleasant restaurant by the water's edge, shaded and airy; then the road dives into a forest of greenery — oaks, banana-trees and orchards. This rustic calm is countered by the mysterious aspect and the awe-inspiring character of the steep, proud slopes on each side.

The sort of country where imaginings vaguely connected with the gods constantly threaten the precarious pleasures of man (who, incidentally, has not hesitated, in his philistine naivety, to instal a hideous, out-of-place match-factory there!), was well suited to religious inspiration and the birth of myths. For here it was that Venus-Astarte and Adonis experienced their passionate love.

The wild valley comes to an end in the grandiose cul-de-sac of Afqa, which is reached by a very spectacular road which follows the upper edge of the right-hand slope and is constantly providing surprise views of precipices, tectonic caprices of Promethean games. Not a moment of monotony, nor even mere prettiness, replaces nobility and grandeur. And yet, wooded slopes alternate with arid ones in accordance with the presence or absence of the water concealed in the mysterious sub-soil of the mountain.

The road, which had moved away from the crest of the Nahr Ibrahim valley, begins, after Kartaba, to follow an increasingly tortuous path to arrive at the source of Adonis. Here, the mountain reveals itself in all its hostility — vertical walls and bare rocks to which a few meagre bushes and tufts desperately cling to give further evidence of the rejection of life.

The grotto of Adonis

And here it is, from this place of silence and death, that this abundant source gushes forth, quite unexpectedly, and becomes red with the ferruginous earth torn from the mountainside in the springtime. Out of death comes life — mysteriously. Hence, no doubt, the myth of Adonis, which is only another version of the myth of the eternal return.

Another surprise awaits the present-day visitor. For when he has climbed

*At the source of the Adonis — nowadays the Nahr Ibrahim —
and invitation to the lustral bath.*

Previous page: *Port, castle, town and mountain... Jbail provides
a sort of summary of the history of Lebanon.*
(Photo NCT.)

the few dozen yards of rock which separate the road from the overhead cavity, which is well below the proud head of the cliff, this black hole, this open grinning mouth in the mountain-side, the size of which had disappoint-ed him (particularly if he had in mind the words of Renan: "one of the finest sites in the world"), he will discover, once he has set foot inside it (which he can only do in summer) that it has the proportions of a cathedral. It was a mouth all right, but with a gigantic throat behind it, the dark vault of which is reflected in an enigmatic lake of cool, blue water.

At the foot of the fall, above the pool which receives it, by the side of which, of course, there is a café, the Romans had built a temple which is now nothing but a heap of ruins. Here were celebrated feasts in honour of Adonis, the handsome young lover of Venus-Astarte, and these feasts included — as can be imagined in the case of those who wanted to experience this myth of love, death and resurrection — scenes of sacred prostitution.

Naturally, such pagan goings on aroused the holy wrath of the zealous, austere Christians who preached the asceticism which so often in Lebanon took the form of using the grottoes as hermitages. And here was the grotto of Afqa being used for an unbridled debauch, albeit a sacred one! The indignation of the holy men, and particularly of the monks of the neighbouring monasteries, was cer-tainly responsible for the practically total destruction of the little temple of Adonis.

And yet, the grotto of Afqa, a sacred place if there is one, still nourishes superstitions. At springtime, people still come and rejoice and lament at the sight of the river coloured with the blood of the God who was loved by the Goddess of love. And the withered fig-tree which has grown at the foot of the ruins of the temple bears, caught in its branches, strips of cloth — sordid rags which, in fact, are a witness to the thankfulness and cries of distress of sick and disabled people and childless women imploring the eternal God with the many faces all confused in the radiant and triumph-ant, but also vulnerable and mortal beauty of the lover of Venus-Astarte.

Altitude: 1,250 m.

Itinerary: 74 km from Beirut. Tripoli road as far as Nahr Ibrahim (31 km). 500 m further, road fork towards Kartaba.

Accommodation: Kartaba, *Villa Rivoli* (com-fortable, pleasant hotel with wonderful view), and six more modest hotels.

■
AAMATOUR, see Chouf.
AQOURA, see Laklouk.

*The superimposed columns of Anjar rise against the blue sky
like a wonderful stage setting.
(Photo NCT.)*

anjar

■ As fragile as stage scenery and light as the dream of a Sultana, the slender columns crowned with pigeons reach up one above the other to the blue sky in the midst of the uniform, silent plain, warm, gilded silhouettes shuddering in the light and hardly distinguishable from the ochre slopes of the mountain. There is something unreal about the way Anjar rises up scarcely 2 kilometres from the Damascus road, at the foot of the Anti-Lebanon. The flat rich plain and the short straight road, in a country where every other journey involves a series of giddy curves, give no warning of this apparition. There is a feeling of unreality; but also of fake. This too perfect quadrilateral of ruins — almost a square (385 metres from north to south and 350 metres from east to west) in the midst of farmland and poplars really is contrived geography taken a bit too far. The visitor feels this so much that he remains for a moment unaware of the pathetic beauty of this rather chaotic site (the excavations, which began in 1953, will still take many years to complete).

A devastated town

But from this vast field dotted with capitals of all sorts, bits of columns and hewn stone, through the middle of which there is a wide avenue (a second of the same width intersects the first at right angles) we gain an impression of the unusual. Unusual, Anjar certainly is for the tourist visiting Lebanon, on account of the blinding clarity of its lay-out and its unity. Whereas in all the other archaeological sites the buildings of different epochs and different civilizations are superimposed on one another, Anjar is exclusively Arab. Anjar is a devastated city. Little is known of its short life, and even the dates are controversial, but it lasted only a few decades. Whether, as some

say, it was destroyed by an earthquake or by man or by both, it disappeared in the eighth century. Subsequently, it would appear to have sunk beneath the soil of the Bekaa. Barely twenty years ago, the land over the middle of what had been a fine fortified city of the Ommiads was still being ploughed.

In fact, the discovery of Anjar — or rather the identification of the ruins found there in spite of the fact that most of it was covered by cultivated land — was the fortuitous result of a search for the capital of a Roman kingdom called Chalcis of Lebanon or Coele-Syria, and the ruins of Anjar were at first thought to be the remains of this mysterious capital.

However, a more detailed examination revealed that it was a fortifiend place founded in the second half of the seventh or beginning of the eighth century. Excavations were continued; what could be built up again was built, and there appeared the outline of a town which must have been a princely dwelling and a caravanserai — resting-place for caravans coming from Damascus to the east and Tyre and Sidon to the west.

A princely caravanserai

Anjar was built with elements taken from Byzantine and Roman buildings (except for the bricks which, alternating with the stone, protected buildings against earthquakes — a characteristically Byzantine technique) by Byzantine architects and craftsmen. This explains the initial error of the archaeologists and the heterogeneous nature of capitals, columns and foundations.

Anjar is a four-square town. Strictly divided into four equal parts by two wide avenues (20 metres) at right angles with a central cross-roads — the tetrapylon, with its four groups each of four columns at each corner — the town had four main gates at the four cardinal points. There is evidence of a great palace formed of two symmetrical wings between which was a courtyard 40 metres square, indicated by columns surmounted by Roman arches; the mosque is separated from the palace by a narrow alley, with a pool in the middle of the courtyard and a smaller palace which was probably the harem. The residential quarter and the marketplace, an empty space where the beasts of burden of the caravan were herded, occupied the western half of the town.

To judge by the exceptional number of stores (more than 600) that have been discovered, Anjar must have been a flourishing and commercially prosperous town. The urban facilities included a system of sewers which was discovered beneath the centre of each of the two great avenues.

How could a place as extensive and well fitted out as this have completely disappeared? For the site of Anjar was well chosen; nearly, only one mile to the east, is the main source of the Litani, where there is water in abundance and where today an almost exclusively Armenian village stands. Here too the streams ripple through the cafés, and vast quantities of trout (raised by the Ministry of Agriculture) swarm in the poplar-shaded pools full of aquatic herbs, while the ruins of Anjar swelter in the sun.

Name: Anjar is probably derived from the Arabic *aïn jarr* (bubbling spring).
Open from 8.30 a.m. to 12.30 and 2 p.m. to sundown. Admission free.

Itinerary: 56 km from Beirut on the Damascus road. Sign-post to left 10 km after Chtaura. The ruins can be seen from afar.

Accommodation: Chtaura
1 hotel**** and 1 hotel***; at Zahlé, 1 hotel***, 1 hotel** and 12 hotels*.

Camping: Vert Bocage, road from Damascus to Deir Zenoun.

Anjar, a ruined city, stands out from the arid slopes of the Anti-Lebanon.
(Photo NCT.)

baalbek

■ The most marvellous tourist site in Lebanon! Baalbek's reputation is such that, for the uninitiated tourist, Lebanon *is* Baalbek. The vast complex of Roman ruins in this small town of 10,000 inhabitants located to the north of the Bekaa at the highest point (1,150 m) of this plateau, has always impressed the traveller. The Romans liked things big; the "small" temple of Baalbek, the temple of Bacchus (built about 150 A.D.) is much larger than the Parthenon, and nothing in the whole of Roman antiquity was so vast, so lofty or so sumptuous as the "great" temple, the temple of Heliopolitan Jupiter.

The Phoenicians and Lamartine

But why Baalbek? In this area, the Bekaa is no longer the luxuriant plain we find at the middle of the plateau. These are rolling dry lands producing poor harvests. And yet, from this not very hospitable country, Baalbek emerges like an oasis of verdure: everywhere are orchards, poplars, pines, green fields and lawns surrounding and penetrating into the small town which always seems to be having a gay time. And there are springs, pools and gardens with those marvellous open-air cafés occupying huge spaces crowded with happy people on Sundays. The Romans of the days of Augustus could not have done better than to build a number of splendid temples visible from so far away, so as to impress local imagination with irrefutable evidence of the greatness of Rome.

The choice was all the more felicitous in that the Canaanites had erected, at an uncertain but very remote date, a temple to the Sun-God who provided life-giving water, the Egyptian God Hadad identified with Baal, and to his partner, Atagartis; hence the Phoenician name Baal-Bek, or town of Baal. The Greeks, after Alexander's conquests, recognized the Sun cult and

Baalbek, the antique site of the country which is most
frequented, is the high point of any journey to Lebanon.
(Photo NCT - Yetenegian.)

called the place Heliopolis (town of the Sun the name which the Romans adopted after their conquest of Syria in 64 B.C. Baal was identified with Heliopolitan Jupiter and Atargatis with Venus. Thus it was that the religious complex of Heliopolis-Baalbek, dedicated to the Heliopolitan triad Jupiter-Venus-Mercury, begun under Julius Caesar and planned at its definitive scale by Augustus and treated with infinite care by the Syrian Emperors (hexagonal courtyard of the temple of Jupiter completed under Philip the Arab, Emperor from 244 to 259), continued to increase in majesty and richness of decoration. The iconoclastic fury of the Christian Emperors of Byzantium, the military considerations of the Arabs, who made a fortress of it, and the effects of earthquakes had reduced the grandiose city of Baalbek to a vast heap of ruins ("We wander through the ruins", wrote Lamartine in his "Voyage en Orient") before the archaeologists of the present century came to restore it and the Lebanese authorities made it one of the chief centres for international tourism, with the organization of an international festival of plays, music, dancing and folklore.

Colossal but subtle

At Baalbek, the visitor will find the sort of crowds which accumulate at all the famous places in the world. But while queuing up for admission, he can gain an impression of the vastness of these temples, for they dominate the small town from an artificial platform — a veritable Acropolis. This explains the 51 steps (reconstructed) in 3 flights which give access to the Propylaea. The *great temple of Jupiter* rises 7 metres above the other buildings and 13 metres above the surrounding gardens. The foundations of the walls on which it rises consist of enormous blocks. Three of

The very rich decoration of the miraculously well preserved temple
of Bacchus borders on the excessive.
(Photo NCT - Yetenegian.)

them are more than 10 metres long, 4.34 metres high and 3.65 metres wide. The visitor, therefore, is scarcely surprised when, a little later, he is shown the largest freestone in the world, at the foot of the hill of Sheik Abdallah at the south-west entrance to the town. No doubt, it was intended for the temples, but was not detached from the rock. It is 21.5 metres long, 4.2 metres high and 4.8 metres wide. The local people call it the "stone of the pregnant woman" (Hajar-al-Hubla).

The temple of Jupiter is both colossal and subtle. This building, which was 89 metres long and 50 metres wide (without stairs and terraces), is preceded by a vast rectangular courtyard 135 metres long, which in turn is preceded by an odd hexagonal courtyard 60 metres in diameter. The six lofty columns of the portico which remain, rising up against the background of Mount Lebanon, combine in themselves this vastness of dimensions (21.5 metres including base and capital) and this precious elegance which is asserted by the extraordinary wealth of decoration of the entablature — a wealth unceasingly rediscovered in the fallen fragments and in the decoration of the pools and of the exhedrae of the courtyards.

The result is that, in spite of their dimensions, the temples of Baalbek are not oppressive. They have grandeur allied with a somewhat decadent beauty, which manifests itself with an unheard-of luxury in the small temple, known as the temple of Bacchus, which is in a remarkable state of preservation. At night, by the light of the projectors, this temple can be seen suddenly arising from the shadows, resuscitated by the blinding whiteness of the artifical brilliance which picks out the details of the carved stones. In summer unfortunately, the scaffolding and stages installed for the festival shock the visitor by their incongruity. But only let him attend one of these shows, and the evocative power of this magnificent background will soon make him forget the disappointments of the daytime.

The mausoleums

At Baalbek, the visitor will find picturesque and animated souks, and if his thirst for old stones has not been quenched by his visit to the "Acropolis" and the ruins on the other side of the road where there is a round temple to Venus of an extremely original design, he can go and see the remains of the grand mosque (its columns were taken from the neighbouring temples) 150 metres east of the Propylaea behind a screen of trees, and a few mausoleums — Kubbat Duris, a round building supported by eight columns at the start of the road to Beirut, Kubbat Khola, opposite the Syria and Lebanon Bank, and Kubbat al-Amjad, an odd rectangular building surmounted by a circular edifice, which may well not be a mausoleum. All these buildings, too, seem to have been built with stone coming from Roman temples. Scarcely any wonder, then, that the temple of Mercury has entirely disappeared, apart from the remains of a stairway.

Name:	Phoenician origin meaning Town of Baal.
Open	from 8.30 a.m. till sundown. Admission LL1.
Altitude:	1,150 m.
Itinerary:	89 km from Beirut. Damascus road as far as Chtaura, thence clearly sign-posted to Baalbek.
Accommodation:	2 hotels***, 1 hotel** and 5 hotels*.
Camping:	La Source (Ras el Aïn).

BEAUFORT

Name:	This was given by the lords of Sagette who in turn assumed the title of lords of Beaufort. In Arabic it is called "Shakif Arnoun" or "Qalaat ech-Shakif"
Altitude:	600 m.
Itinerary:	85 km from Beirut, 42 km from Saida. Take the road to Nabatiye, 9 km after Saida. Then ask.
Accommodation:	At Saida, 4 hotels.

beaufort

■ The austere road from the coast which leads through a chaos of huge blocks of limestone and little green fields of tobacco to an even more desolate countryside reveals to the traveller, at about 40 kilometres from Saida, a strange excrescence on the mountainous eastern horizon.

This is the castle of Beaufort dominating, by means of steep slopes in one of the wildest possible positions, the river Litani which, hardly 2 kilometres further on, abruptly changes its direction from north - south to west. From Beaufort, there is a view of peerless beauty and grandeur. Nothing, for miles and miles around, is lost to view. The lord of Sagette-Saida made a good choice of the best strategic situation for his *Qalaat-ech-Shakif*. The ruined castle itself would be disappointing if it were not for the fact that a kind of anguish and giddiness emerges from the shade of its broken-down underground halls and from the blinding light of the esplanades covered with the invading grass. Beaufort was originally an Arab edifice which was seized by Foulque of Anjou, King of Jerusalem in 1139, and which the lords of Sagette converted into an impregnable fortress. In 1192, one of these lords, Renaud de Sagette, waged a long battle against Saladin whom he esteemed and admired. The Sultan Baybars recaptured it in 1268. After a siege, the castle capitulated with 22 knights and 480 men. It also sheltered a large number of women and children. So it is probable that about a thousand people found refuge in the fortress. Some of the interior fittings of the castle, which enabled so many people to live there, are still quite visible.

SALADIN AT BEAUFORT

This happened in 1189. Saladin, who had swept from victory to victory, arrived in front of Beaufort where Renaud de Sagette was in defense with a large force of men. This Frankish nobleman, knowing how precarious was his position, requested a parley. He offered to deliver up the castle, on the understanding that he would be guaranteed a residence in Damascus and a grant. But, he added, a delay of three months would be necessary to enable his family, who had remained in Tyre, to be placed in safety, and also to take his harvest with him. Saladin agreed, but Renaud had thought of this subterfuge in order to gain time to reinforce his defence and to make preparations for a long siege.

Ar first, Saladin did not believe in this duplicity on the part of a Frankish nobleman with whom, despite the hostility which separated them, he enjoyed discoursing. An Arab historian once wrote "He sustained a number of discussions with us in defense of his religion, of which we proved to him the falsity. He was an agreeable man to deal with and his conversation denoted a cultivated spirit". However, the time passed and Saladin called upon his adversary to deliver up Beaufort. Renaud, who found himself in Saladin's camp, called to his soldiers, in Arabic, to yield up the castle but, at the same time, told them in French to resist.

This episode has naturally inspired many historians, both Arab and Frank. The version that I have given was presumably that of the former. As regards the others, they gave a very poor opinion of Saladin's reputation for chivalry.

HENRI-PAUL EYDOUX
"Châteaux fantastiques, vol. IV"
(Flammarion, Paris)

becharre

■ The cedars, the famous cedars of Lebanon, the "cedars of God" *(Arz el-Rab)*, the thousand-year-old cedars which are the emblem of the Lebanese Republic, are the cedars of Becharre. It is to them that this town, which has become a fashionable winter-sports centre, owes its reputation. This pretty well-to-do little town is perched on a slope at the end of the Kadisha valley, the holy valley, at an altitude of 1,400 metres. It is the last town in this famous valley, formerly the refuge of so many Maronite hermits (some still remain today), which the visitor has followed either from Edhen by the north road from Tripoli or from Kousba by the south road from Chekka. Both roads have a large number of magnificent view-points: the Kadisha alternates between arid slopes and verdant pastures, wild precipices and soft-rolling terraces. At its source, beyond Becharre, an awe-inspiring circle of bare ochre-coloured mountains closes the horizon. The bottom of the valley guards its hospitable freshness and verdure, which provide a large number of springs, in spite of the overhanging rocks. To the right of the *route des Cèdres* (the cedars road), the visitor can go on foot along a path over the flank of the steep valley, which will offer him admirable view-points overlooking the Qadisha valley and lead him to the *grotto of Qadisha*, a fine stalactited cave at the bottom of the valley.

The town of Gibran

Becharre was the birthplace of Gibran Khalil Gibran (1883 to 1931), the greatest Lebanese writer in English. The royalties from his very fine book "The Prophet", published in New York in 1923 and translated into 30 languages, were left by the author to his native town and bring in 100,000 dollars a year. The visitor is therefore greeted by posters proclaiming "Becharre, the town of Gibran". On the second floor of a building in the town is a Gibran Museum, with a collection of the canvases and sketches of this writer who was also a painter, and souvenirs of his lifetime. These sombre pictures, with their arabesques of intertwined nudes, recall both the drawings of William Blake and the oneiric painting of Odilon Redon. Sign-posts show the way to Gibran's grave, not far from Becharre.

The "cedars of God"

From Becharre, a good road which includes two or three absolutely vertiginous hairpin bends leads to the cedars, 7 kilometres away.

These patriarchs of the forest, these hermits of the high places which only attest their sombre presence where nothing else can grow, number only about 300 today owing to the extent to which this resource of Lebanon, made famous by Egyptian hieroglyphics, the Bible and Babylonian cuneiform characters, has been exploited.

Cedar wood was the most sought-after of all woods in ancient times on account of its resistance to decay. The Lebanese cedar fittings of Cheops' barge, discovered near the great pyramid of Giza in 1954, were marvellously well preserved after 4,400 years, and it is even said they still retained their pristine odour. Egyptian documents dating from 2 600 B.C. tell us that Pharaoh Snefru (IVth Dynasty) imported forty cargoes of undressed timber for boat-building from Byblos. The sovereigns of Sumer and Babylon purchased Lebanese cedar, as also did Solomon for the building of his temple.

Today, the dark clump of old cedars is religiously guarded. The Maronite Patriarch has for a long time been protecting the "cedars of God", of which it was said in the Psalms:
" The trees of the Lord are full of sap,

The cedars of Becharre are the "Cedars of God" — a
thousand-year-old treasure jealously guarded by the Lebanese
authorities.
(Photo M. Guillard.)

The cedars of Lebanon, which he hath planted."

The Lebanese Government has now made itself responsible for their protection. The cedars are huddled together at a height of 1,900 metres with a small chapel in their midst. It appears that only about a dozen are more than 1,000 years old, though some of these have reached the age of 1,500. The young ones are only 200. In this connection, it is interesting to note that a 200-year-old European cedar is the same size as a 1,000-year-old Becharre one, but its wood is a long way from having the hardness and resistance to rot of the old Lebanese cedars grown on the arid rock. These great trees with their dark foliage which give the quite unexpected feel of velvet are serious in their isolation and in the sort of unshakable rejection which they tacitly pronounce. It is a religious seriousness, both protecting and threatening. They are austere mountain-dwellers who intend to be respected, and the notices asking visitors not to deface these venerable trees seem ridiculously superfluous. There is so much sovereign power in their outstretched arms and their old bodies like those of Saurians or ageless pachyderms that one wonders what sort of dim-witted persons could have carved their names on them.

The "Cedar of Lamartine"

One of these graffiti (a notice indicates the cedar of Lamartine) is supposed to have originated from the poet and his daughter Julia, whose names are in fact carved on the trunk. But Lamartine stated that he could not get to the cedars and had to be content with contemplating them "from five or six hundred paces away".

The religious gravity of the cedars of Becharre makes a strange contrast with the soft, sensual sweetness of the yellow slopes which dominate them and can be seen through their foliage.

To the roof of Lebanon

When you are under the foliage of these disconcerting cedars, you feel them watching over you with the supreme assurance and redoutable vigilance of great raptores watching their prey. But once you leave them for the chalets and hotels of the "Cedars" winter-sports centre 1 kilometre away or better still take the teleferic to the pass from which a ten minutes'walk brings you to the other slope of the Lebanon dominating the Bekaa, the forest of cedars dwindles to the size of a small troop of frightened animals clustered together. The teleferic terminus is a good starting-point for climbing the *Kornet es-Saouda* (3,088 metres), the highest peak in Lebanon. Two hours of not very strenuous walking are recompensed by the most awe-inspiring panoramic view of the country, from the sea (where Cyprus can be seen on a clear day) to the Bekaa, the Anti-Lebanon and the Syrian desert.

Name: it was called Buissera at the time of the Crusades.

Altitude: 1,400 m; the Cedars 1,900 m, winter-sports centre 2,000 m.

Itinerary: 115 km from Beirut. Tripoli road as far as Chekka (66 km), then "route des Cèdres" (well sign-posted) via Amoun, Kousba, Hadeth ej-Jobbe and Hasroun.

Accommodation: 1 hotel***, 2 hotels** and 1 hotel*. At the Cedars: 2 hotels***, 5 hotels** and 2 hotels*. At Haddeth ej-Jobbé: 5 hotels** and 1 hotel*. At Hasroun: 2 hotels**, 1 hotel*.

■

BAROUK, see Chouf and Jezzine.
BATROUN, see Rachana.
BEDDAWI, see Tripoli.
BYBLOS, see Jbail.

beit-chebab

■ At about 20 kilometres from Beirut, in the Metn, the village of Beit Chebab, with its narrow, winding streets going up and downhill, offers a peaceful and shady respite.

This is a village which has retained centuries-old crafts — weaving (though few precious fabrics are still woven) and simple, ordinary pottery. The movements are the same as those of the multitude of European potters who claim to be reviving, though not without artifice, a lost art. Here, however, they still retain the moving humility of movements which have never been forgotten. At Beit Chebab can be seen a curious kiln which is so old that nobody knows when it was built.

Master bell-founders

But there is another most unusual craft which has continued in this same place for centuries, practised by the same family. This is a craft which is very jealous of its manufacturing secrets — bell-founding. Only to a few privileged persons (or to those who are considered too ignorant of these things to be able to act as spies) does the head of the firm — a very affable man, full of ingenuous but legitimate pride — open the doors of his workshop, with its blackened walls and its heavy tackle blocks festooned with sturdy chains. On the floor are lined up the refractory clay moulds for bells of different sizes.

The special feature of these bells, which this craftsman emphasizes, is that, even though some of them exceed half a ton in weight, they are all cast in a single piece and not in two halves, as, he says, is the case in Europe. In accordance with the proportions handed down from father

Two crafts flourish at Beit Chebab bellfounding and pottery.

to son, he mixes together the tin and copper of his bronze, taking care to impart to each bell the sound which will be recognized by the faithful.

Beit Chebab's reputation for the manufacture of bells has long since gone beyond the frontiers of Lebanon. Thus, the master-founder has just received an order for a bell for a church in Bordeaux. However, his chief customers are the Christian villages of Lebanon. Bells are ordered with a specific pitch. From valley to valley, the bells echo on; they engage in a conversation; they speak, call to one another and proclaim their friendship or their hostility. "Listen to what the bells are saying," old people say to the children. They call: *"r'au je lahaun!"* (come here) or say: *"Ruhu min haun!"* (go away). And in this dark den which appears to have come straight out of the Middle Ages (but the son, who speaks excellent French, is studying technology), the foreigner, thinking of all this, achieves a firmer grasp of the complex unity of this disconcerting Lebanon, the homogeneity of which is based on the resolution of contradictions which are more superficial than deep-lying, and the final product of which still has flaws which are more evident than real.

Name:	Arabic, meaning "house of the young".
Altitude:	750 m.
Itinerary:	20 km from Beirut. Tripoli road as far as Antelias, then Bikfaya road; after 5.5 km, turn left for Beit Chebab.
Accommodation:	Beirut.

beit ed-dine

A thin cool stream of water such as lulled the meditations of Bechir the Great.
(Photo Marinier.)

beit ed-dine

■ From Deir el-Qamar, the former capital of the Lebanese Emirs abandoned by Bechir II, the *palace of Beit ed-Dine,* built on a rocky spur dominating a steep, precipitous valley, is only a small white spot in a mass of greenery. Above it is a series of fine terraces, the winding lines of which seem to trace the contours of the mountain. A wonderful site, where the Lebanese mountain, with astounding variety, assumes its most contrasting charms — grandeur and grace, wildness and sweetness, aridity and freshness.

Bechir the Great, whose "reign" (1786 to 1840) was marked by so much cruelty, crime and cunning, in addition to so many vast designs and admirable achievements, made an excellent choice. In the very heart of this Lebanon which, in a more lasting manner even than Fakhreddin, he unified, he spent thirty years, until his deposition in 1840, in building, enlarging, embellishing and decorating this admirable Oriental palace. The whole is a synthesis of Byzantine and Arab traditions, Ottoman and Italian influences and specifically Lebanese features.

A palace for the pleasure of the eye

Once he has gone through the door, the visitor, who was expecting an austere closed space, finds himself in a vast courtyard — the *maidan,* with wide openings onto the valley and the horizon of mountains behind which can be felt the presence of the sea. Beit ed-Dine is a palace organized so that those who live there have pleasant views. A second courtyard, approached by a zigzag corridor lined with stone benches, also opens generously onto the south-west. A pool, from which rises a thin jet of water, is situated in the middle of it.

Two vast double staircases, a majestic portal decorated with a mosaic of

The Emir held court in this great hall hung with velvet.
(Photo NCT.)

different-coloured marbles, and a first floor with elegantly-arcaded galleries supported by slender columns form the heart of the princely habitation. The reception halls, sumptuously decorated with marble and carved wood throughout, are with their velvet draperies, of extreme luxury. If we are to believe Lamartine, this sumptuousness did not extend to the guest-rooms: "Our rooms," wrote the poet, "although in this magnificent palace, would have appeared too dilapidated to the poorest of our cottage-dwellers — the windows were not glazed — a luxury unknown in the Orient in spite of the severity of the winter in these mountains; neither beds nor any other furniture; just bare, decrepti walls, full of rat and lizard holes; the floor was just uneven earth mixed with chopped up straw."

Feasts and meditation

And now there is spread out before the visitor a display of the thousand and one nights which recalls both the splendid feasts with their many-coloured costumes and the peaceful, solitary evenings during which the lord of the palace smoked his narguileh in the long hall — the *liwan*, which opens on one side onto the patio where the fountain plays.

Here we sense both a place of silence and a place of tumult. The silence of meditation and the tumult of the feasts and the games, when hundreds of horsemen rode round the great courtyard, as Lamartine saw them from afar before arriving at the palace. But it is in the most intimate parts of the palace that luxury assumes the ambiguous dimensions of solitary joys — in the harem and in the hammams. The latter, illuminated by a multitude of glass cabochons fitted into the cupolas, are distinguished by a wealth of decoration of extraordinary subtlety. Next to them are the rest-rooms with mastabas on which

have been placed the reclining models of women dressed in the costumes of the period, with the tube of the narguileh in their hands. Beit ed-Dine is the official summer residence of the President of the Lebanese Republic. A *palace* in the same style, that *of the Emir Amine,* son of Bechir, was built on a promontory dominating Beit ed-Dine. This palace which enjoys a magnificent view of the valley, the mountain and the palace of Bechir II, has been restored by the Lebanese National Tourist Council and the Lebanese Department of Antiquities, and converted into a luxury hotel with 24 bedrooms, 9 of which include a drawing-room giving direct onto the patio.

Deir el-Qamar

A visit to Beit ed-Dine is necessarily preceded or followed by a visit to Deir el-Qamar, capital of the Emir Fakhreddin and residence of the governors of Lebanon from the sixteenth to the eighteenth centuries, which still retains in its pretty little town square several palaces of the seventeenth and eighteenth centuries. The village, with its red-tiled roofs and terraces and the fine convent which overlooks it, would be an epitome of all the virtues and beauty of the Lebanese mountain, had not urban civilization in the form of week-end houses, and stereotyped, villas come to disrupt the profound harmony of centuries.

Names : Beit ed-Dine means "house of faith". Deir el-Qamar means "convent of the moon".

Beit ed-Dine open from 8.30 a.m. to 12.30 and from 2 p.m. to sundown. Admission: LL1. *Deir el-Qamar* seraglio open from 8.30 a.m. to 12.30 and from 2 p.m. to sundown. Admission free.

Altitudes : Beit ed-Dine, 900 m. Deir el-Qamar, 860 m.

Itinerary : 44 km from Beirut. Saida road as far as Nahr ed-Damour, then road to Deir el-Qamar (40 km from Beirut). Good roads.

Accommodation : Under construction : Beit ed-Dine 2 hotels**. Aïn Zhalta (19 kms) 3 hotels**.

*At Beit ed-Dine, a few charming details which demonstrate the
enlightened taste of the Lebanese Prince who lived there in the
first half of the nineteenth century.
(Photo NCT.)*

The only real plain in Lebanon—one of liquid purity.
The Bekaa, situated at an altitude of 800 metres.
(Photo Almasy.)

bekaa (region of the)

■ A well-ironed patchwork quilt, green, red and yellow with a surface as calm as that of a still lake. That is the first impression of the Bekaa for the visitor who, having left Beirut, has just crossed the *Baidar pass* at an altitude of 1,556 metres, with its depressing bare crests and its sour aspect.

With his eyes still full of the generous greenery of the large gardens of the well-to-do villas of Sofar, the last collection of summer residences before the pass, the visitor has no time to abandon himself to melancholy at leaving behind him the fine plane-trees which lined the road before, suddenly, like a grey sky opening to admit the blue, the mountain opens up onto this joyful luminosity. At first sight, the Bekaa is a spread of liquid. Never till now has Lebanon provided the visitor with such an abstractly flat and horizontal surface. The caprice of the rapid, winding descent to Chtaura widens, shrinks and hides this image. At last, the area widens out, extends to north and south, becomes populated and full of orchards and coppices. The picture on the easel becomes a fresco. Nicolas de Staël becomes Pissarro.

A liquid plain

The Bekaa, this high plateau varying in altitude from 800 to 1,150 metres, is very beautiful, and so unexpected. And here it is, enclosed between the eastern flank of the Lebanon and the western flank of the Anti-Lebanon, matching its colourful opulence with the unworldly, hostile aridity of the rough slopes of the mountain which, on a summer afternoon, assume very delicate mauve and pink pastel shades which render them ethereal. Nor are the steep eastern slopes of the Lebanon, which border the Bekaa to the west, much more hospitable with their thin, unhealthy vegetation. The Bekaa is 120 kilometres long and its width varies from 8 to 15 kilometres. The Beirut-Damascus road cuts through the middle of it, where it is most fertile and best exploited. This is the granary of Lebanon.

Flat and bare, the Bekaa has no trees or very few — some orchards, a few planes and poplars, and a tiny pine forest (a coppice, in fact) near Aamiq in the south, the only one on the entire plateau.

The roads, perfectly straight, cut through fields and vineyards where climbing vines alternate with those whose plants creep along the ground like monstrous serpents hiding their heads under the shades of the leaves. Tractors have appeared, and the visitor might think himself in Europe or America were it not for the presence, next to the conductor, of a passenger shading himself with an umbrella.

Agriculture has caught up with industry in the Bekaa. Thus, in addition to a small factory for the assembly of tractors on the Damascus road a few kilometres from Chtaura (flanked by two other factories, which are non-agricultural), huge long, low white buildings, out of place in this landscape, occasionally appear. These are the batteries where poultry are subjected to a scientific treatment which fattens them rapidly and speeds up the laying process.

The southern Bekaa

The Bekaa is not long in becoming unfaithful to the first impression it gave. The serene opulence of a liquid plain gives way, to the north and south, to drier, more broken land, which in the north is totally arid. Crops give way to pasture. For the Bekaa is also the sheep country. These sheep, with their wide, heavy tails, are driven in endless Indian file by shepherds who in the south ride peacefully along on donkeys, and in the north are wild and armed. The Bekaa soon stops being as flat as it appeared at first. To the south, it loses its peaceful assurance and rises, in a more broken relief, towards the Lebanon.

The road from Chtaura ' to *lake Qaraoun* which runs along the foot of the mountain, lined with willows, pines, acacias, and cypresses, reveals a number of pretty villages on the left — Qabb Elias, Aamiq, Khirbet Qanafar, Saghbine — hidden in the foothills. To the right, there is the triumph of water proclaimed by the greenery of the Bekaa. The smooth plateau hollows out and becomes concave before closing round a blue patch in the green and ochre — lake Qaraoun, the dam reservoir of the Litani, the chief river of Lebanon, which runs exclusively through Lebanese territory.

The wild Bekaa

The national project for the Litani will give the chief advantage to the western slopes of south Lebanon, which it will supply with electric power. But the dam and the lake should also allow of the intensification of cultivation in the southern Bekaa and put the region on the same level as the centre which is well supplied with water. For the essential problem of the Bekaa is one of water, or rather of a more rational use of the water which the Bekaa is not lacking thanks to the immense reservoirs constituted by the Lebanon and the Anti-Lebanon. For in the Bekaa there are a large number of springs, including those which feed the Litani, which runs toward the south and the Orontes which flows to the north.

It is true that, between the two rivers and even further south, the Bekaa rises, and its more tortuous relief, which is but a faint reminder of the placid central plain, culminates at Baalbek at an altitude of 1,150

metres. Baalbek, incidentally, is a veritable oasis on account of these lovely springs.

All around it, the Bekaa is arid, although the northern part of the plateau has much more rainfall than the south. But in any case, from May till October, rainfall is practically zero. Exploiting the whole of the Bekaa is a problem of irrigation: a problem which has been solved in the centre, is being solved in the south, but is completely in suspense in the north.

This fine Lebanese plateau between the two mountain ranges of the country, which links up with the Homs depression in the north and, after crossing through particularly wild country where there is more bare white rock than arable land, extends into the fault-scarp of Jordan to the south, has always been an attraction for men of all epochs. Even the seafaring Phoenicians, who scarcely ever went further than the coastal plain, came to the Bekaa, as is proved by the very name of the plateau and of Baalbek.

Fertility, geographical situation (a major natural highway from Asia Minor), climate — everything made the Bekaa propitious for receiving men. The present-day tourist particularly appreciates the bracing dryness of the atmosphere after the humidity of Beirut. But it is very hot there in summer (though the nights are very fresh and even cold) and fairly cold in winter. However, excellent hotels at Chtaura and Baalbek, provide all the comfort made necessary by such climatic conditions for the molly-coddled bodies of most of our contemporaries.

Name: Phoenician in origin.

Altitude: 1,000 m average.

Itinerary: From Beirut to Chtaura by the Damascus road. From Becharre to Baalbek by the Ainata pass. From Jezzine or Lake Qaraoun via Marjayoun.

Accommodation: Baalbek, Chtaura or Zahle.

beyrouth
(beirut)

The Pigeon Grotto, one of the characteristic places on the Beirut coast, is a favourite spot for outings among the inhabitants of the capital.

*At this end of the Ras Beirut, the corniche is bordered by the most
modern buildings.
(Photo NCT.)*

beyrouth

■ The octopus city. A town eaten up by its suburbs whose tidal wave of concrete already hides the coast from Khalde to the bay of Jounie. The monstrous development of Beirut is a terrible factor in the lack of economic, social and psychological balance of the country. There are no recent official statistics, but estimates dated November 1970 give the population of the Lebanese capital and its suburbs as 795,000, out of 2,126,000 for the country as a whole. It is said that, at certain peak hours, two thirds of the entire population of the country is in Beirut. Everybody agrees that, today, the population exceeds one million. In a few years, *Ras Beirut,* a practically deserted cape, has been covered with vast modern buildings, the serried ranks of which have taken this rocky promontory by storm.

The Grotto of Pigeons

At the point of the promontory there is a site of very Mediterranean picturesqueness — that of the curious rocks of the *grotto of Pigeons*. The seashore promenade (Avenue de Paris and Corniche Chouran, now Avenue du Général de Gaulle), which extends as far as this pleasant spot, has been for a long time the place for embassies, the magnificent campus of the American University of Beirut, and the restaurants and cafés in the neighbourhood of the grotto. But behind the curtain of well-shaded luxurious residences there was nothing. Today, a vast new town covers this plateau of sand which runs smoothly down to the series of fashionable beaches to the south.
Beirut leaves you with a muscular souvenir in your calves and your back. In your calves because of the unceasing climbing up and down the winding streets from the sea up to the narrow plateau, where they straighten out and become monotonous. In the back because you have survived the

aggressivity of the Beirut drivers for whom the pedestrian appears to be a negligible quantity.

As nearly all streets are one-way, since they are so narrow, a motorized Lebanese worthy of his standing as the most prosperous citizen of the Middle East will drive through them at full speed, skidding gaily with screeching tyres as he carves his labyrinthine passage. And since apparently the pavements of Beirut are reserved for parking, the pedestrian's lot is not a happy one. In actual fact, everything works out all right, for the ferocious monster which threatens you will stop dead if you step into the road.

The flight to the west

Beirut is no longer hidden in the hollow of the beautiful *bay of St Georges,* a magnificent natural shelter where the installations of the harbour were built. It scarcely spreads any more, as formerly, towards the foot of the mountain into the coastal plain, which is relatively wide here but not much more than 4 or 5 kilometres. It covers the western extremity of its vast balcony, whence it looks towards the north and, having crossed the Nahr Beirut, the bed of which is today of ugly cement, gnaws away at the coast along the road to Tripoli, where some little factories are situated.

Since scarcely a decade ago, the centre of Beirut has ceased to be near the harbour, around the populous and colourful *Place des Martyrs* — the official name of a square which everyone calls the *Borj* (Arabic for tower, since there was once a tower there) or the *Place des Canons.* Of course, the business, administration and political worlds have not entirely deserted this part of old Beirut (the Parliament House is there, at the Place de l'Etoile) which still continues to attract the visitor, even if, sometimes, a young Beirutian, too finicky about

the reputation of his town, reproaches him for photographing this too vigourously Oriental spot with no apparent signs of wealth. "Go and take a snapshot of Hamra," he will say.

Ostentatious wealth

Hamra is the new commercial quarter, with prosperity in the Western style, 2 kilometres west of the Borj where, every few seconds, the incessant noise of traffic is drowned by the shriek of jet planes landing at the nearby airport of *Khalde.* All that you see of the Orient there are curiosity shops where the visitor can buy richly ornamented Damask cloth, engraved copper trays, worked leather cushions, coloured glassware, narguilehs, and so on.

The wealth of Beirut is intentionally ostentatious. And since there really is a lot of wealth, the ostentation is appalling. Ultra-modern buildings arise everywhere.

Vast commercial centres raise their enormous, smooth, black masses. The first of these, the Starco, incidentally, is situated in the lower part of the town, in old Beirut. And above all there are the great hotels rivaling one another in size and luxury (the latest, the "Holiday Inn", overtops, with its 25 floors, its enormous, blinding white rival, the Phoenicia), all of them crowded into a space of several hundred metres at *Minet el-Hosn,* the geometrical site of the night life of the well-to-do. The oldest of the night spots and the only one situated on the sea shore — the one which, according to the devotees of the Beirutian life of pleasure, is the most select — is the Saint Georges. A Hilton was recently built half way between Minet el-Hosn and the harbour on an avenue planted with palm-trees.

But there is also a less ostentatious form of wealth — that which has made Beirut one of the great financial centres of the world. The Banks have not emigrated to Hamra, with the notable exception of the Bank of Lebanon. They have remained in the old quarters, not far from the Place de l'Etoile and near the Post-Office. They are all there. Some of them still have their old, agressively ochre-coloured pre-war buildings in the old streets which give onto the harbour, such as Rue Allenby, but many have bowed to modern taste with imposing modern buildings, compact masses of marble, metal and glass. These giant safes, symbolical of Lebanese wealth, are grouped in a street lined with buildings; this is the Rue des Banques.

The death of old houses

The building fury which has overtaken Beirut is making the city uniform; it is gradually losing its former specific character and assuing the monotonous anonymity of all great cities throughout the world. In the plane from Paris to Beirut a young Lebanese asked a wealthy Arab from Kuwait used to living in Beirut, what he thought of Paris: "Paris? Just like Beirut — only larger." He wasn't so very wrong.

Formerly, the residential quarters of Beirut were not like those of Paris. The fine old Lebanese houses of the nineteenth century with their red roofs, ochre walls, colonnades, multiplicity of triple ogives, curious little pediments, and balconies of stone or forged iron shaded by a fragile awning — a mixture of Byzantine, Arab and Italian influences — used to prepare the visitor for the satisfaction, both for the mind and the eye, of seeing the houses of the mountain, incorporating the same architecture and the same colours, so

A BRIEF HISTORY OF BEIRUT

Beirut formed part of the semi-independent Phoenician League, in which were comprised the coastal towns, of which Gebla (Byblos) had taken the lead.

Commercial and cultural contacts of Beirut with Greece developed, and the prosperity of the town was not affected by the Roman conquest of Syria in 64 B.C. It obtained the status of Roman city. It became "the Latin island in the eastern Hellenic sea".

As from the third century, Beirut became the seat of a law school whose renown was equal to that of Athens and Alexandria.

In 551, the town was destroyed by an earthquake.

In 635, it was captured by the Arabs.

For two centuries, from 1099 to 1291, the Crusaders and the Arabs fought for possession of Beirut.

In 1516, it fell under the domination of the Ottomans and only recovered a passing prosperity on two occasions; once under the regime of Emir Fakhreddin (1585-1635) and later under Bechir II (1781-1840).

In 1840, Beirut fell under the control of Mehemet Ali, and was bombarded by the Anglo-Austrian-Turkish fleet.

After 1860, a great influx of refugees (especially Maronites) swelled the population and the town recuperated its activities.

In 1920, Beirut became the capital of Greater Lebanon, under French mandate.

perfectly inserted into the landscape. It was like a call from the pines, the cedars and the orchards. Now, every day that passes sees some of these fine dwellings disappear at the hands of the demolition contractors.

Fortunately, a considerable number still remain, such as the one which contains the *Sursock Museum* — a private museum of modern art. Such fidelity is a costly vanity, for the offers made by the building promotors are increasingly attractive, and the tidal wave of concrete, marble, glass and aluminium seems irresistible. You should look at these old houses for a long time and feast your eyes on these havens of grace and sweetness, still protected by fine trees, as you appreciate the precarious rest they offer to the beholder.

Incidentally, there are in the Lebanese capital a score of very fine Arab palaces which their owners have artistically restored, making veritable museums out of them.

Segregation on its way out.

For those who are not disgusted with the first, deceptive impression of aggressive, boring modernism, Beirut has many surprises and marvels in store. It is a microcosm, a compendium, of Lebanon as a whole, and its geography illustrates the demographic complexity of the country. Formerly, Beirutians used to group themselves by confessions. This state of affairs is a long way from being abolished, but the quarters where people of all origins and all religions mix freely together are gaining ground. This is the case with all the new, wealthy or well-to-do quarters. However, to the north of the city, *Achrafieh,* an old working-class district which is becoming modernized and bourgeois, and *Saint Nicolas,* a traditional, high-class district, are exclusively populated by Christians, whereas *Basta,* to the east, has an

exclusively Moslem population. In the suburbs, to the north, *Borj Hammoud* is exclusively Armenian as a mere glance at the signs of the shops will tell, while *Borj Brajneh* to the south-east and *Ouzai* to the south are Moslem. At the periphery of the town, the Palestinian refugee camps constitute another demographic element.

The wrath of nature and the vicissitudes of history have combined their efforts with man's determination to renovate in effacing almost completely from the face of this historical old city all vestiges of the past. The terrible earthquake of 551, followed by a tidal wave, almost completely destroyed Beirut, and this work of destruction was completed by a huge fire in 560. True enough, columns may sometimes be seen rising unexpectedly from the subsoil, revealing, after the demolition of a relatively old building, the ruins of a far more ancient one.

The national museum

But after all, if you are looking for Phoenician, Greek, Roman or Byzantine antiquity in Beirut, you must look for it in the *National Museum.* This noble building, opposite which there is a very graceful Herodian column, somewhat perplexes the visitor with its Pharaonic facade, but it is extremely rich.

The very spacious presentation of archaeological items, maps and explanatory diagrams make a visit to it easy and pleasant. In the vast hall, surrounded by fine marble sarcophagi found at Tyre, on the sides of which are inscribed, with Hellenic grace, fine old legends such as that of Achilles, there sits the foremost exhibit of the museum — the sarcophagus of Ahiram, king of Byblos in the thirteenth century B.C. bearing the first inscription in the phonetic alphabet of 22 letters.

This remarkably pure Ptolemaic head is one of the most touching relics in the Beirut Museum.

The museum contains some very fine Byzantine mosaics including that of the "good shepherd", very well preserved, covering an entire wall. In the basement, there is an impressive series of anthropomorphous sarcophagi. On the wall opposite them, the appealing head of a woman of the Ptolemy epoch is watching them. One entire hall has been devoted to the reconstruction of a Byzantine tomb decorated with frescoes.

The halls devoted to pre-history and proto-history, with their bronzes and pottery, recall the extent of an unbroken past. The visitor will examine with curiosity the ichthyoliths, or fossilized fishes, displayed in the stairway, but he ought to know that they are offered for sale in certain grocery shops at Ehmej in the caza Jbail.

Phoenician art

He will undoubtedly be more interested in the objects connected with customs and religions on the first floor — strange axes of latticed gold, and Phoenician statuettes and jewels which will give him a clearer idea of a little known civilization which, as a result of its geographical position, was subjected to such diverse and such vast influences, that it produced this amalgam, so disconcerting to the classifying mind.

In this respect, the new halls on the first floor, inaugurated on 28 June 1973, are very enriching. Here can be seen, carefully lined up in a display case, those strange bronze figures covered from place to place with a gold leaf (beginning of second millenium B.C.) which appear to advance in ordered ranks like an army.

A visit to the Beirut museum is an indispensible complement to any visit to Tyre and Byblos. The museum stands aristocratically apart from the

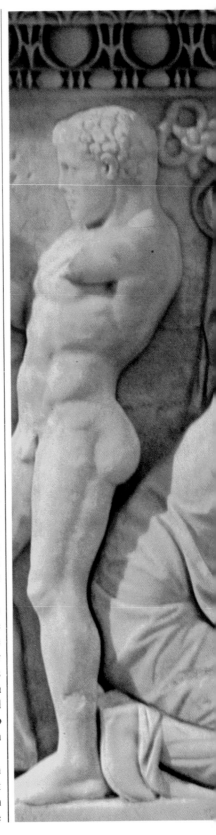

*This detail of one of the finest sarcophaguses found at Tyre
shows Priam supplicating Achilles.*

teeming city, in the southern part, almost touching the race-course and not far from the splendid pine forest which is supposed to have been planted by the great Emir Fakhreddin during the seventeenth century in order to hold down the sand which was threatening the town. The visitor can make an intermediate halt in time before going back to his air-conditioned bed-room by going for a walk in the district of the Borj or Bab Edriss, which will restore to him Oriental eternity in all its richness and colour.

The great mosque

If he is still pursued by the demon of history, he will go and look at the great *mosque of Jamii el Omary*, which was formerly the church of St John the Baptist of the Knights of St John of the Hospital, built during the first half of the twelfth century on the site of a Byzantine church (of which the crypt has been discovered), which in turn was built on the remains of a Roman temple. It is a fine example of a religious building of the time of the Crusades. The apse, which gives onto the corner of two little streets behind Rue Mosquée Omari, suddenly surprises the visitor with the sight of a Romanesque church chevet such as he might have seen in Auvergne; the interior, however, which is whitewashed throughout, will bring him back to Islam in spite of its evident church structure.

Old Beirut

First, the visitor would be well advised to mingle with the crowds in the *Place des Canons* itself, which is the terminus of a whole lot of bus lines and all the "service taxis" circulating inside and outside the town; then the *souks* — narrow streets, frequently roofed — where you are carried along

*The variegated, colourful street markets of Beirut teem with an
extraordinarily intense and picturesque life.
(Photo Marinier.)*

by the crowd; these souks formerly contained all the small traders and each street had its speciality — vegetable and fruit market, clothing market, goldsmiths' market, etc...

Many well-to-do Beirutians come from the residential quarters to do their shopping here, even if the articles offered for sale are ''made in Germany'', ''made in Italy'', or ''made in France''. Craftsmen are conspicuous by their absence. The souks of Beirut are for selling things. People often come here just to drink a lemonade or a fruit drink or taste the pastries or other dainties which they eat as they walk along.

All the souks are situated to the north of Bab Edriss and on the west side of the Place des Martyrs (but it appears they are going to be transferred to the superstructures of the new section of the motorway from Tripoli near the harbour). The east side of the *Place des Martyrs* also provides a good dose of the picturesque, with the little streets of the red light district where each apartment bears a sign in Arabic and Roman characters consisting merely of a woman's first name. The *Borj* district is also that of the local cabarets, though the belly dance does not come up to the sophistication of the Crazy Horse Saloon in Paris. Here too cafés with backgammon players and narguileh smokers, are unpretentiously picturesque. Half way between these places, where the tourist hardly ever goes, and the fashionable night-haunts and bars of the Rue de Phénicie at *Minet el-Hosn,* the Avenue des Français, which leads to the harbour, provides a motley assortment of more or less shady joints. But if he takes any of the little streets running north from this same avenue, the visitor will find huge typically Lebanese restaurants overlooking the sea (the coast is rocky at this point); these are well-run establishments where he can eat excellent local dishes, particularly those made from fish.

To get about in Beirut, the simplest and most economical method for anyone who has noted the various itineraries is the ''service taxi'' (standard charge of 25 piastres). There are, of course, buses which the Beirutian, for some obscure reason, considers it beneath his dignity to take, and ordinary taxis. But the majority of the latter have no meter, and stuck to the windscreen is the embarrassing notice ''insist on the official charge for the journey'', which comes to the same thing as making anybody who does not know the town thoroughly comply with the driver's demands. It is therefore better to agree on terms beforehand. In case of dispute, it is best to take the number of the taxi and inform the tourist police, who are very well organized; the driver will be brought to your hotel

the next day. However, taxis are not expensive.

But the stranger may find himself in an embarrassing situation, for the user of any means of transport is supposed to have an exact knowledge of his destination (the name of the owner of the building may be very helpful). Drivers know the names of only a limited number of streets, and numbers mean nothing to them. The consequences of this situation are not as catastrophic as might be imagined, for the Lebanese is very helpful and talkative. He will put you right.

At the *Beirut Lebanorama* (boulevard Hadath Chiah) there is a total of 5,000 square metres of mock-ups showing the chief historical monuments of Lebanon in their original state. This may be of interest to the visitor who has not troubled to examine the ruins closely. However, for the person who is interested in history and the plastic arts, it gives an impression of a doll's house and a set of play-blocks in a Christmas shopwindow.

Name: The Phoenician name is unknown; Latin name Berytus; French Beyrouth.

National Museum: Open every day except Monday from 9 a.m. to 12 and from 2 p.m. to 5, from 1 October to 31 March and from 9 a.m. to midday and 3 p.m. to 6 from 1 April to 30 September. Admission: LL1.

Lebanorama: Open every day from 8 a.m. to 8 p.m. Admission, LL1.

Itinerary: See Part Three: "How to get to Lebanon".

More than one hundred tourist agencies, camping sites.

Khalde Airport, 7 km away.

All facilities and resources of a very modern city.

Accommodation: A large number of hotels of all categories, including 24 hotels****.

Accommodation in surrounding district: See chapter «The Lebanese Journey» for list of hotels under Aaley, Aajaltoun, Aaramoun, Baabdat, Baalachmay, Beit Mery, Bhamdoun, Bikfaya, Bmakkine, Broummana, Chiyah, Dhour ech-Choueir, Hazmiye, Khalde, Maameltein, Naas, Rayfoun, Sofar, Souk al-Gharb, Tabarja.

Camping: University Centre, Damascus Road, Beirut.

The goldsmiths' market
a permanent temptation.

chouf

■ Name pregnant with history. A curious and attractive region in the very heart of Lebanon, including Deir el-Qamar, Fakhreddin's capital, and Beit ed-Dine, palace of Bechir II, the Chouf is the cradle of Lebanese unity. It offers a bewildering variety of attractions and considerable human interest. The alert eye is constantly attracted by some marvel or other. The mountain is successfully adorned with all the varying seductions of gentle wooded slopes, rich terraces, pleasant valleys and springs of cool water, such as the beautiful, restful *waterfall of Ain Mourched*. But it also displays the austerity of its wild grandeur and the desperate, inhuman bareness of its high cliffs. And to the south, the white scar of its limestone rocks stands out from the tiny, fragile, obstinacy of the green terraces.

Moukhtara

One of the centres of the Chouf is *Moukhtara*, the land of the Jumblatts, whose immense palace almost disappears in the surrounding orchards (apple and nut-trees); this village is perched high in a very Mediterranean scenery. Four huge yew-trees in the courtyard of the palace hide its imposing dimensions. This Arab-style dwelling of the late eighteenth and early nineteenth centuries symbolizes the feudal power of a great progressive lord who is a redoubtable political dialectician as well as a mystic devotee of esoterism and Hinduism to whom practically everything within sight belongs. But many other villages impregnated with the silhouettes of men in *shirwals* wearing a tarbush with a white band, the distinctive sign of the Druze holy man, confront the visitor with a sight of their simple clean homes and their terraces surrounded with climbing-vine. Sometimes, an old deserted house of yellowish stone, decorated with the Druze symbol of the lion,

such as the *Abu Chakra house* at *Aamatour* and the grandiose remains of the vast *palace of Ali Pasha Jumblatt* at *Baadarane,* inscribes the history of the last two centuries in a context which seems eternal. On the forlorn peak of a burnt mountain which prodigiously dominates the entire region, far from any human habitation, was built the *khalwa* of *Aamatour,* over which a high-ranking *okal* (wise man), of great wisdom and courtesy, watches. From this high point, the geography of the entire Chouf can be seen as from an aircraft. To the north, much lower, are the red roofs of Moukhtara. To the west, at what appears to be a great distance, are the hills flanking the valley of the Nahr el Awali, which rises there and runs into the Mediterranean a few kilometres north of Saida. To the south, are the cliffs of Niha pierced by the Shakif Tyron. And to the north-east, there are the dark masses of two great cedar forests, Masser-ech-Chouf and Barouk.

Nabi Yacoub

Further south, below Niha, after a long and winding climb, you come to a curious sanctuary that of *Nabi Yacoub,* the tomb of the prophet Jacob, the very old and modest dome of which (the keeper has not the slightest hesitation in informing you it dates from the time of Moses) is perched on an extraordinary height. Inside, the walls are covered with velvet and gaudy coloured embroideries, while the tomb itself is covered with the same sort of decoration. This is a sacred place of pilgrimage for the Druzes who have built up around it a sort of caravanserai. But the sanctuary of Nabi Yacoub is also venerated by Christians.

Itinerary: Moukhtara is 52 km from Beirut, via Beit ed-Dine. Aamatour is 4 km from Moukhtara, and Niha is 8 km from Aamatour.

Accommodation: Beirut or Deir el-Qamar.

fakehe

■ On the road from Baalbek to Hermel, among the first steep foothills of the Anti-Lebanon, take the road to the right just before the one leading to Ras Baalbek, and you will find, isolated on the outskirts of the Bekaa, the little village of Fakehe, perfectly white against the red of the rocks, which courageously tries to climb that hostile deserted mountain. Only an occasional fig or mulberry-tree breaks the terrible bareness of the scene.

It is a matter for wonder how these people live. They weave carpets, or at least some of them do, and this silent work, carried out in narrow dark workshops, is scarcely the sort to animate the surroundings. Here you will see six women — young ones, not so young and old ones — crouching down to work together on the same high-warp loom. They do not say a word. They pass the woollen thread through the shed of the warp well above the finished portion, and then, with a vigorous beat on the wooden comb, force it down onto the stock. These are high-pile woollen carpets with geometrical or floral patterns imitating those of Persian carpets.

The proprietor of the workshop, his wife, his daughter and female relatives offer a cup of coffee to the interested visitor, show him their finished carpets, and engage in a long conversation, glad of the break in this desert of silence. They are particularly proud of tapestries representing naive portraits. "We'll do your portrait," they say. They live comfortably, and the little courtyard giving onto their house is scrupulously clean. It contains a magnificent cherry-tree — a touching luxury in this desert village.

(See note p. 130).

The Jumblatt palace dominates the lovely village of Moukhtara with its imposing mass.
(Photo NCT.)

fakra

■ "The most extensive ruins of Mount Lebanon," Renan said of the temples of Fakra *(Qalaat Fakra)* in his "Mission en Phénicie". The enthusiasm of the author of "La Vie de Jésus" (he wrote his book in Aamchit, a village not far from Jbail) has been tempered for the present-day visitor by the considerable number of ruined Roman temples which he can see in Lebanon.

Nevertheless, here is a truly remarkable collection consisting of a *large temple,* perhaps dedicated to Adonis, then lower down a *small temple* dedicated to Atargatis, and further on the *tower of Claudius,* which looks like a small fortress in ruins, together with a large *altar* and a pretty little *tabernacle.* But it is the surrounding landscape which makes a majority contribution to the interest of the site.

Limestone hemp

Dominating the rich valleys of Kesrouan with their luscious orchards, it is encrusted in strange grey rocks imitating vegetable shapes which might have been cut horizontally by the scythe of some demiurge. Temples, tower and altars seem as if they had halted a huge tidal wave of limestone hemp. This field of half-harvested mineral plants obsesses the sight. It can be seen through the ruins, between the columns...

Limestone dolomites in fantastic shapes, they were already visible with their immense scene of romantic ruins some 10 kilometres to the west. Before Raifoun and as far as Faitroun they could be seen appearing, disappearing and appearing again, a monstrous, apocalyptic chaos of strange petrified vegetation, baroque columns, odd buildings torturing the landscape, natural elements ready for the adoration of successive gods — sacrifice tables, altars, and entablatures of temples — before these were even thought of.

Before visiting the ruins of Fakra invaded by the limestone flood, and after having passed Faraya, the big winter-sports centre, the visitor could have seen, 4 kilometres away, another curiosity — the *natural bridge of Nahr-al-Laban,* which is so perfectly symmetrical that it is almost unbelievable it was not the work of men.

Name: The full name is Qalaat (or Kalaat) Fakra.

Altitude: 1,300 m.

Itinerary: 60 km from Beirut. Turn right at Rayfoun in the direction of Mazraat Kfardibiane. Thence a not very good road to the left to Fakra. Distance via Faraya, 65 km. Same road as far as Rayfoun, but from the "Faraya Mzar" Hotel, take the road to the source of the Nahr al-Laban. Thence, 3 km of unmetalled road to Fakra.

Accommodation: At Faraya, 1 hotel **** (with heated swimming pool), 1 hotel ***, 3 hotels ** and 6 hotels*. At Kfar Zebine, 2 hotels** and 1 hotel*.

FAKEHE (see note p. 129).

Altitude: 900 m.

Itinerary: 39 km from Baalbek on Hermel road. First right after Jdaide (2 km).

hasbaya

■ In the valley of the Wadi-Taym, cradle of the Druze religion, at the foot of Mount Hermon, the highest peak in the Anti-Lebanon, the village of Hasbaya is wrapped in silence and reserve. Here is an atmosphere of silent dignity, open-heartedness and warm hospitality.

At the highest point of this village built on the side of a hill, at the end of a courtyard shaded by a huge oak, a tree almost always associated with the sacred, is the *khalwa,* one of the oldest in Lebanon. These meeting-places of the Druzes are not normally open to visitors, but sometimes the *okals* (wise men) allow strangers inside, providing they are not just ordinary tourists but are motivated by an authentically human interest. Inside there is a place of prayer and meditation, covered with carpets and with low divans running the length of the bare walls, while there is a curtain separating this large and quite impersonal hall from the khalwa reserved for the women. Men are seated on the divans in such simple silence that it has a strange effect. It would be difficult to find a welcome more profoundly impregnated with serene and fraternal dignity. In the scarcely more animated street outside, the silence of the mountains becomes even more tangible.

At Hasbaya, weavers make the red coats with white stripes of the Druzes. Down at the bottom of the village there is the *palace of the Chehabs,* now being restored. This is a huge ochre-coloured building, austere and powerful as a fortress; the portal is decorated with two lions, the emblem of the family.

For anyone who knows the history of Lebanon, this place of silence and peace nevertheless recalls one of the most bloodthirsty episodes in the

This little tabernacle with a statue of Kalat Fakra rubs shoulders with a curious jumble of dolomitic limestones.

hermel

fratricidal struggle between Druzes and Christians in 1860. The Commander of the Ottoman garrison had 900 Christians brought here under a promise of protection. Then he disarmed them and opened the gates to the Druzes, who massacred them. Two or three kilometres further down flows the *Hasbani,* one of the three watercourses which form the Jordan. Like all the rivers of Lebanon, it allows a charming vegetation, which makes a remarkable contrast with the arid austerity of the surroundings, to grow on its banks. As always in such a situation, the visitor will find one of those immense cafés nestling amid the foliage and flowers, where the water, under the control of man, murmurs through channels, leaps up in fountains and rushes down waterfalls, while the sun shining through the branches reproduces the joy of a Renoir painting.

Name: From the name of the river Hasbani.
Itinerary: 125 km from Beirut via Chtaura and Lake Qaraoun.
Accommodation: Chtaura, Zahle or Jezzine.
Since 1967, Hasbaya has been a military zone; only visitors with a permit issued by the military authorities are admitted.

HERMEL

Names: Hermelos was the name of a Christian king of the northern Bekaa during the first centuries AD, according to an Arabic manuscript.
Deir Mar Maroun, the convent of Saint Maron, founder of Maronism.
Altitude: Hermel, 780 m, crest road culminating in 2,000 m.
Itinerary: 144 km from Beirut. From Baalbek (55 km), take Homs road, fork at Ras Baalbek Station (Mhattat Ras Baalbek), where there are sign-posts.
Accommodation: Baalbek.

■
CHEKIF TIROUN (Shakif Tyron), see Chouf and Jezzine.
DEIR EL-QAMAR, see Beit ed-Dine.
DEIR MAR-MAROUN, see Hermel.
ECHMOUN, see Saida.
FAYTROUN, see Fakra.

■ Among the arid, reddish rocks, on which grow a few scattered prickly bushes, a shepherd dressed in a faded military tunic with his head enveloped in a checkered scarf places the butt of his very long old rifle on the ground and loads it with a huge ramrod which he thrusts into the muzzle. Through the same landscape walks a young man with a revolver wrapped in a white cloth at his belt. This is Hermel. Hermel, the region of which the small town of the same name is the administrative centre, is in a way the Far-West of Lebanon — a mountainous country far from inhabited centres and government authorities. This does not in the least mean that the visitor is in danger; the population has a very strict sense of hospitality, generosity and honour. But he may very well be surprised when, on the difficult road running up the eastern side of the Lebanon from Charbine to Ainata and thence along the crest, he suddenly sees an armed man rising out of the ground beside him as he comes to a halt.

The banks of the Orontes
This desolate country which is in prolongation of the Bekaa to the north is a sort of rolling desert supplemented by a particularly wild and hostile mountainside.
Hermel itself, a peaceful town perched on a height, is of no particular interest to the tourist, but 2 kilometres before reaching it on the way from Baalbek, he crosses the Orontes, here known as the Nahr al-Assi, on the banks of which are a number of shaded, fresh café-restaurants, filled with the murmuring of the water, where it is so pleasant to relax to the strong odour of meat being broiled in the open air, while entire families busy themselves with the preparation of complicated dishes, chopping up the parsley, killing and drawing chickens, and preparing delicious sauces…

The pyramid of Hermel (Quanouat al-Hermel)

He who crosses this desert discreetly cut in two by the gorge of the Nahr al-Assi is rewarded by two discoveries. About 10 kilometres before Hermel, about 600 metres to the right of the road and visible for miles around, is the *pyramid of Hermel*. This is a strange monument which, isolated as it is in the middle of a red desert covered with blocks of black basalt gives a false impression of its size, for this odd landmark on which are engraved hunting scenes and whose origin, date and purpose are a matter of dispute, is nothing more or less than a huge boundary mark. As we approach it, we realize its size — it is 27 metres high. According to the most generally accepted theory, it is the sepulchre of a Syrian prince of the first or second century B.C.

Continuing along the road to Hermel after leaving the pyramid, we find, 2 or 3 kilometres further on, on the left, a narrow road which leads to a place quite near to the *Grotto of Saint Maron (Deir Mar Maroun)* which dominates one of the sources of the Orontes. In the grotto, carved in the rock 200 metres perpendicularly above the source, the founder is supposed to have lived as a hermit a considerable part of his exemplary life. Below, in the hollow of the valley with its steep, bare slopes, the *"blue source" of the Orontes,* in which an astute café proprietor keeps his bottles of pepsi-cola cool, forms a tiny pool of crystalline water surrounded by trees, which act as a gracious escort to the Nahr al-Assi as it flows through its narrow gorge away to the north.

Beyond Hermel, the road turns towards Charbine, loses its asphalt

Unexpectedly in the middle of a real desert, rises Quanouat al-Hermel, the pyramid of Hermel.

jbail (byblos)

and becomes increasingly rough, flinty and sandy. However, the motorist, unless he is worried about his nice new car, will manage to reach without difficulty, at a distance of 7 or 8 kilometres (the road follows the Wadi ech-Charbine), the *steles of Nebuchadnezzar*. There are two of them, one on each side of the wadi. The scarcely legible inscriptions (all the more praise to the archaeologists who deciphered the incredible boastings of the Babylonian king!) are engraved on the rocks hollowed out in the form of a niche.

Further on, the road which rises steeply, gets worse and worse. A few kilometres beyond the steles, it divides into two branches which join together again a hundred metres further on. This is the moment of truth for, whichever branch you take, you must be very careful. From then on, the road to Ainata presents plenty of difficulties but none which are insurmountable. There is even asphalt in one or two places.

However, do not expect to find any service stations in this area. It is absolute desert. There are goats, lots of them, though you see no goatherd. However, if you stop, there he is suddenly, his rifle by his side.

The vegetation becomes sparser and sparser, and the horizon broadens into soft, rolling slopes. The road roughly follows the crest of the eastern slopes of the Lebanon, which can be seen in all their savage desolation. The bare earth of the heights is scattered with spots of stunted bushes, among which, occasionally, a dark, thick juniper-tree can be seen in its twisted agony. This is the grandeur of the Hermel.

(See note p. 132.)

■ The oldest town in the world. This is a claim disputed by Jericho, though the latter cannot boast such a series of superimposed layers of history. Men have lived here in a community for 7,000 years, without interruption, and have founded towns here since 3 000 B.C.; these have been built one on top of the other as the centuries passed. This small rocky promontory 40 kilometres to the north of Beirut, dominated by the proud ruins of the Crusaders'castle and surrounded by the mediaeval town with highly picturesque souks, reveals to the perplexed tourist an open space of 5 hectares, in the lines of the low walls and excavations of which he will try in vain to read the prodigious history of Byblos.

The excellent monograph written by Maurice Dunand, the archaeologist who has been in charge of excavations here for over half a century, will be an invaluable guide. If he reads this little book in advance, he will avoid a lot of misconceptions, and a second reading, after his visit, will then bear full fruit. The little folder brought out by the Lebanese National Tourist Council can also constitute a good introduction for the less demanding.

The patient work of archaeologists

The mound of Byblos is not very spectacular because everything apart from the powerful castle of the Crusaders and a small Roman colonnade is more or less flat on the ground. And yet, the archaeologists have taken great pains to clarify the historic structure of this site. They have even gone as far as to transfer to a distance from the place where they were built certain monuments which covered previous ones in order that both could be seen. This is the case with an Amorite temple built above another temple consecrated to an unknown divinity.

*The castle of Byblos watches over the sea through Phoenician
and Roman ruins.
(Photo M. Guillard.)*

Moreover, the three last surrounding walls, together with their platforms, are very clearly discernible in the northern part. And the joy of solving this archaeological puzzle is a reward for efforts which not even the flock of tourists can impede. The latter are much too occupied playing hide and seek in the labyrinth of the Crusaders castle to wonder about the L-shaped temple or the neolithic sanctuary.

But this place of grass and wild flowers, with its few trees swept by the wind, is an incitement to meditation. Time comes up and hits you. You feel as if you are sucked down into the swamp of time, no matter whether you walk through the strange *temple* with its *obelisks* (the masseboths which aroused the fury of the biblical prophets) and the *altar* raised in the centre (which makes you think uneasily of human sacrifices), or whether you make your way cautiously down to the *royal tombs* of the second millenium B.C., where the curiously horned sarcophagi watch from the depth of their galleries, or whether you look at those enormous jars of red terra cotta with an opening on the side, which acted as tombs (the corpse was introduced in a crouched position and the jar sealed up afterwards).

The town of Osiris and Adonis

Here, from neolithic times to the twentieth century, women have come to draw water from the same source as the one which can be seen at the bottom of a craggy slope today. Here, from the third millenium B.C., the Egyptian vessels seeking the good wood of Lebanon, particularly the incomparable cedar, came to moorings. Here was buried, in the thirteenth century B.C., Ahiram, king of Babylon, whose sarcophagus, now in the Beirut Museum, bears the oldest extant inscription in the phonetic alphabet, the alphabet inven-

Byblos. This place full of wild grass and wild flowers, with its few trees swept by the wind from the sea, is propitious to meditation.
(Photo Almasy.)

ted by the Phoenicians. Byblos also gave its name to a book — the Bible. The civilization of this town, apart from the extensive use made of papyrus, symbolized the knowledge of antiquity.

Here the coffin of Osiris was disembarked. Here, no doubt, was born the legend of Adonis. The cult of Osiris and the legend of Adonis are both based on the feeling of adoration by men of the death and resurrection of nature marked by the annual cycle of the seasons. Byblos was the town of Adonis, and the divine mistress of the handsome young man doomed to violent death was, no doubt, initially Baalat Gebal, the "lady of Byblos" (who presided over the destinies of the town for more than 2,000 years); the ruins of her temple show that, before becoming Astarte, she was the Phoenician Goddess of love, later identified with Aphrodite or Venus. Jbail is the Gebal of the Bible (the inhabitants of Byblos were known as Giblites). The Greek sailors called it Byblos — a corruption of the word *papyros*, the Egyptian "paper" of which they found abundant supplies in this port. The fact is that Byblos maintained close relations with the inhabitants of the Nile valley as from the first dynasties of the Ancient Empire. During the Middle Empire, it was officially considered an Egyptian town by the government of the Pharaohs. Countless Egyptian objects have been discovered in the tombs of the necropolis. They can be seen in the Beirut Museum.

The Crusaders' castle

The Crusaders called Byblos Giblet. They conquered the town in 1104 and immediately started to build a fortress which was subsequently modified by the Arabs, who took it for the first time in 1266 and then for good in 1291. The enormous stones with which the castle was constructed were probably not cut by the Crusaders but taken from old Roman or Phoenician buildings. With its enormous vaulted halls and its staircase cut into the wall of the donjon, this ruin is imposing on account of its grandiose character. From the terrace the visitor can attempt to make out the lay-out of the successive ancient towns, clearly marked out by the excavations.

The town itself, with its fine old narrow souks, its pleasant little port reached by a very steep road and, above all, the *church of St John*, a fine specimen of Romanesque twelfth century architecture, flanked to the north by a curious and graceful baptistery, is well worth a visit. Scarcely has the tourist crossed the threshold of the church when somebody will suddenly appear and offer to guide him, giving full details of its history, waxing indignant about the way it was treated by the Turks when they garrisoned it, and listing all the miracles performed by Saint John Maron.

Byblos constitutes a sort of condensed history of Lebanon. Here you come very close to the stupefying imbrication of peoples and civilizations who lived, fought and died there, sealing with their joy, suffering and blood the intertwined destiny of these people who had come from the desert and the sea and who ended by forming a people of the mountain.

Name: Old Greek name: Byblos. In the Bible: Gebla. At the time of the Crusades: Giblet. Jbail comes from a Semetic word meaning "small mountain".

Open from 8.30 a.m. till sundown. Admission LL1.

Itinerary: 40 km from Beirut on Tripoli road.

Accommodation: 1 hotel*** and 2 hotels**. At Halat, 1 motel**. At Tabarja, 1 hotel**** (with private beach and swimming pool).

Camping: *Les Colombes* at Aamchit (4 kms North) *Mocamp*, Société des Centres Touristiques du Liban.

jeita

■ Delirious nature in the depths of the earth. Venimous effervescences of stone. Enormous orchids of pinkish limestone. Mineral mushrooms in fantastic shapes. A petrified animal with a mad, grinning sneer. A surrealist festival organized by Pluto. A journey to Lebanon is worth while for the *grottoes of Jeita* alone.

Of course, there are plenty of grottoes with stalactites and stalagmites in the world, but it would appear that none of them even approach the astounding wealth or the extent of those of Jeita. Over a distance of 650 metres, at two levels, the lower one in a boat and the upper one on foot, following perfectly made cement gangways, the tourist picks his winding way through darkly forbidding caverns. Sometimes he passes through vast halls the size of a cathedral — some of the grandiose naves seem to contain giant organs or the vast chandeliers of madmen — and sometimes through narrow corridors.

A feast of the imagination

Sometimes the hard reddish floor of the upper grotto is cut up into a kind of lace, allowing the dim light from the lower grotto to penetrate between two curves, the lines and colours of which are an irresistible reminder of the beautiful ochre-coloured terraces which follow the movements of the Lebanese mountain.

The milk-white curve of snowy breasts awakes in the sensual dreamer the ardent peace of fulfilled desires, while a moment later a thousand daggers threaten him as he is watched by monstrous mineral animals and limestone insects the size of dinosaurs crouching in shady corners. Candlesticks and Mexican phalluses and cactus, and innumerable vertical concretions, springing imperiously up, guide the tourist along this road of dreams.

The most striking, the most spellbinding, is the upper grotto, where there is only an occasional drop of cold water to remind the visitor that this Plutonian museum, which defies the imagination, is the result of niggardly drippings which have gone on for thousands of years. It is cool here, but not excessively cold. The work of the divine sculptor with the fantastic imagination is completed once and for all time.

From the whole thing, from the warm tones of the rocks, emanates a sort of underground summer climate, as if this phantasmagoria were warmed by a hidden sun. This impression is accounted for by a very well-devised and discreet lighting system which hides some shapes in the intangible incandescence of a fiery sign and cruelly picks out certain daggers and gnomes' grimaces, leaving menacing caverns of shade and shining lovingly on the knees and breasts of goddesses.

The subterranean river

The lower grotto, full of the noise of water (though the roar of the waterfall at the entrance gives way to an increasingly profound silence as you advance into the grotto), through which you pass in a boat managed by a mariner skilled at sliding through the maze of rocks, lays the damp coldness of its ceiling on your shoulders.

Occasionally, a large drop of water falls on your neck. Here reigns a half-darkness which is suddenly penetrated either by a wide area illuminated like a church on feast days or by discreet lights picking out some opulent flower or martyrized body.

All this, together with the sound of the black water lapping against the sides of the boat, would give a distinct impression of a journey to the nether regions, if only the jolly Charon taking you there, only too well aware of his customers' tastes, would remain silent. He does not, nor do his passengers. Full of good intentions, he shouts greetings to his mates rowing in the other direction. He points to an illuminated form: "Santa Maria!" he tells his cackling tourists. And so they go on, unceasingly pointing out the most idiotic of analogies, reducing this place of profound mystery to the puerile level of a Christmas shop-window, seeing nothing but heads of bulls or lions, toads and towers of Pisa. But you may be lucky enough to chance on a silent boatman and well-behaved tourists. There are some.

From the lower grotto, where you arrived by car, those who are frightened of walking can take the teleferic to the entrance to the upper grotto for an Alice's tour through wonderland. Jeita has caught up with the fashion. The inauguration of the upper grotto was marked by a concert of electronic music given in the grotto itself, the music having been specially devised for the place by François Bayle of the French Radio. That same year, the vaults of Jeita also echoed to the music of Karl Heinz Stockhausen.

Open from 8 a.m. to 12.30 and 2 p.m. to 6 except Monday. Admission: LL2. The lower grotto is closed in winter.

Itinerary: 25 km from Beirut. Tripoli road as far as Nahr al-Kalb, thence Faraya road for 3 km, where there is a sign-post for Jeita.

Accommodation: Beirut.

■
HARISSA, see Jounie.
KADISHA, see Becharre.
KORNET ES-SAOUDA, see Becharre.

The grottoes of Jeita — a Plutonian festival enough to satisfy
the most surrealist visitor.
(Photo Almasy.)

jezzine

■ Jezzine has its waterfall — one with a fall of 50 metres or so — watched by the card-players and narguileh smokers in the line of cafés ranged along the edge of the escarpment at the foot of which the water falls.

Jezzine, the small town which is the administrative centre of the caza which bears its name, is protected on all sides by a circle of hills; at twilight it begins to fill up with people out for the evening and young men who invade the cafés.

Past and present mix well at Jezzine. The craftsmen who make traditional cutlery show in their windows both anachronistic swords and daggers, with their beautifully decorated she-aths, and typically Lebanese table knives with their metal-studded handles.

Jezzine provides visitors with un-troubled peace and a mountainous landscape on a human scale. The setting sun emphasizes the pure line of the peaks with a mauve fringe from which the silhouettes of pines emerge.

The traveller feels this peace very intensely at night, when the mountain all round, which appeared to be deserted in the daytime, lights up with a thousand lamps, and on a near-by hill an immense red cross is illuminated while the vigorous chanting of the tritons is heard.

And yet, the road from Saida had passed through terribly arid and fairly tortured countryside. The projections of huge whitish rocks fought fiercely against the little terraces determined to provide life for a handful of vines.

The road running north from Jezzine soon brings you back to the grandiose. It runs along one of the wildest escarpments that exist — the vertical cliffs of *Jebel Niha*. There, half-way up, 200 metres above the road, at about 5 kilometres from Jezzine, are the strange grottoes which have been converted into fortresses (*Chekif Tiroun*). They were used first by the Druzes, then by the Crusaders, and lastly by Emir Fakhreddin fleeing from the Turks. This extraordinary, impregnable refuge, supplied with spring-water by a piping system (which was poisoned by the Turks to make Fakhreddin come out in 1635), can be reached from the village of Niha by a road which gradually becomes a footpath through this desolate country, and the last 1,500 metres must be covered on foot. The footpath up the side of the cliff, which formerly allowed of the passage of only one man at a time, has now been improved and is no longer so dangerous.

Altitude: 850 m.

Itinerary: 30 km from Saida and 71 km from Beirut. It is also possible to reach it through Beit ed-Dine (34 km). Niha (the village) is 13 km from Jezzine (turn off at Bater, 10 km from Jezzine). Altitude of grotto, 1,100 m.

Accommodation: 1 hotel** and 4 hotels*.

jounie

■ This coastal village which, incidentally, contains a considerable number of fine old houses and beautiful gardens terraced like an amphitheatre on the steep wooded slope of the mountain, is worthy of attention for the magnificent lay-out of its large bay, the finest in Lebanon. It runs round in a curve of such purity that, when you look at it from the high *terraces of the Lebanese Casino* at Maamelteine to the north, its beauty almost takes your breath away. Particularly at night, when thousands of lights shine all up the slopes of the mountain except for a wide zone of darkness below the crest, which can be clearly seen.

Harissa

The *Virgin of Lebanon*, at Harissa, an enormous white statue, attracts many visitors. To be sure, from where it stands there is a very fine view of the bay. A teleferic, starting from the middle of the shore of the bay runs straight to it.

Naturally, among all the abundance of marvels of Lebanon, there had to be a Virgin. The statue, which looks out to the west, turned its face to the south lots of simple, pious people swear that it happened. Down on the shores of the bay, the atmosphere is less religious. The biggest and finest aquatic sports-harbour in Lebanon is situated in the bay. This is *Kaslik* harbour.

Jounie-Harissa *teleferic:* cars leave every 30 seconds. Open from 9 a.m. to 6 p.m. except on Monday. Return fare: LL3.5.

Itinerary: 21 km from Beirut on Tripoli road.

Harissa: Altitude, 580 m.

Accommodation: Beirut, Nahr al-Kalb, Bzoummar, Maameltein, Tabarja.

Jounie sums up the whole of Mediterranean charm.
(Photo NCT.)

laklouk

■ This village, at an altitude of 1,950 metres, is inhabited in the summer by nomadic Arabs from Chekka. This strange, completely isolated village is a collection of low-built houses more than half of which are cafés. There is an unusual and ambiguous atmosphere in this wind-swept place. The only dominating point is a 2,050 metres peak to the east crowned by a statue of the Virgin.

It appears that people come from several miles around to take meals in the village where, in very simple café-restaurants, highly reputed meats are prepared, the animals being killed to order. It is also said that these feasts are usually accompanied by a certain amount of licence.

And yet, Arab el-Laklouk is an end of the world. You can get there from Kartaba (a beautiful village in a fertile area with admirable views against the background of the valley of the Nahr Ibrahim). The direct road provides enchanting, giddy-making views down into the valley. The rich green terraces flow down with the delicacy of a fur pelt.

Another, but longer road runs through Aqoura (sign-posted to the left half way from Kartaba to Afqa), a typical mountain village where there is a precious, abundant spring, to which the villagers go with their jerrycans. From Aqoura and Laklouk, the new, excellent and well sign-posted road (though it is shown on the map as unasphalted), gives a view of the compact, hostile range of peaks to the east, which separate these mountains from the Bekaa.

Winter-sports

Of the two roads leading from this forgotten village, the one to the north goes to Tannourine el-Faouqa and the one to the west ends up at Jbail. The latter descends rapidly to the oasis of orchards, pines and flowers of the fantastic tourist centre of Laklouk, with its large hotel (the Shangri-La) and its bungalows. From this was developed the fine new winter-sports centre of Jebel Laklouk. Further down, the road runs through a wild valley, a sort of canyon with threatening sides.

If, on the other hand, you go towards the north, the aridity continues, and a forbidding cliff restricts the view to the left. A few kilometres further on, you find a natural collection of troglodytic dwellings known as La Bergerie (the sheepfold). This is a curious assembly of oddly shaped rocks isolated in a desolate landscape. Cultivation and livestock reappear, together with the thousand-year-old life of the country and a humble church by the side of the road and a café with its door covered by an awning of branches.

Pot-Holes

Here, the chalky mountain is pierced with impressive pot-holes. Two of these can be reached — one on the left of the road 6 kilometres from Arab el-Laklouk (necessitating a walk of several hundred yards) and the other 500 yards further on, to the right. The first is more spectacular: after a rapid and fairly difficult descent taking about ten minutes (twice that for getting up again), there is a fantastic series of three natural bridges one over the other above an abyss surrounded by rough cliffs where a number of niches appear to have been cut by human hand for the effigies of some unknown divinity or the proud inscription of some conqueror. Owing to its contrasts, the region of Laklouk is one of the most remarkable in the Lebanese mountain.

Altitude of hotel site: 1,700 m.

Itinerary: 70 km from Beirut. Take a well sign-posted road to the left 1 km before Jbail.

Accommodation: 2 hotels***.

The slopes beneath the cedars provide good skiing
(Photo NCT.)

nahr al-kalb

■ The first serious obstacle encountered by the traveller of ancient times following the coast northwards from Palestine was a rocky spur forming the southern bank of the mouth of the Nahr al-Kalb, the river of the dog, the Lycus of the Ancients, on the bank of which, says legend, was mounted the statue of a dog which barked when an enemy approached. The legend, by the way, has a natural explanation. When the wind blows strongly, it forces its way into holes in the rock and produces a growling like that of a dog. Today, a short distance from the Lebanese capital, the motorway to Tripoli runs through this obstacle by means of a tunnel.

Like most Lebanese watercourses, the Nahr al-Kalb is overwhelmed by its valley. It is a matter for wonder that such a small river can have cut such steep gorges. However, the mouth of the river is not lacking in charm with its old bridge, the surrounding reeds, and the café in its greenery. Further up the valley runs into coolness and silence, becomes narrower, and is increasingly threatened by its slopes.

Here, however, the interest is of historical rather than natural origin. As a result of an eccentricity to which it is difficult to ascribe other reasons than strategic ones, conquerors from Ramses II in the thirteenth century B.C. adopted the habit of engraving inscriptions proclaiming their feats of arms in the rock of the natural obstacle to the advance of an army constituted by the steep high hills on the left bank of the Nahr al-Kalb.

A total of seventeen different inscriptions have been traced, all on the left bank except one by Nebuchadnezzar (from 605 to 562 B.C.), which is on the right bank. In addition to these there are more recent plates commemorating the liberation of Lebanon and Syria in June-July 1941 and the evacuation of Lebanon by French troops in 1946.

Some of the steles are beside the road in the entrance to the valley, while others have been engraved on the cliffs overlooking the sea. Today, access is had to these by a stairway, from the limited height of which there is an excellent view of the sea to the north. Some of the steles have been defaced by the successors of the conquerors whose exploits were praised, and the inscriptions have also suffered from the elements. The most legible, of course, are the most recent; they are far from being the finest. The gigantic scriptorium of Nahr al-Kalb includes ancient Egyptian, Babylonian, Assyrian, Greek, Roman and Arab steles.

Name: Arabic words meaning "River of the dog", the Lycus of the Romans.

Itinerary: 14 km from Beirut on the Tripoli road.

Accommodation: 1 hotel**** (with beach and swimming pool).

rachana

■ Almond-trees and sculptures! This tiny village in the caza Batroun is something different. Its slender almond-trees, protected by white limestone walls, submerge it, and in springtime Rachana is dressed in brilliant white.

But trees are not the only adornment of this beautiful village. Everywhere, by the side of the road, in the orchards and in the courtyards, there are sculptures in natural stone, wood and polyester, of a dazzling whiteness or grey as granite from the depths of the ages. This permanent exhibition of sculptures is due to the initiative of the three Basbus brothers whose studio is here, where each follows his own bent, from the praying mantis figurative of the Giacometti style and sensual forms of the Laurens style, to abstract and all sorts of barbarious totems.

Rachana, whence the eye unceasingly encounters the sea beyond the rolling mountains, between the steep valleys, is dominated by the *castle of Smar Jbail* perched on the highest crest — a fortress in ruins whose drawbridge, which has long disappeared, crossed a moat courageously cut out of the rocks.

An extraordinary, legendary castle in which you are continually finding water tanks — the local people say there are two hundred of them. These are narrow, cylindrical tanks the walls of which appear to have been polished by a stone mason who loved his art. The first one, at the entrance to the castle, has magic properties. You lean over the edge and drop a coin into it. When the ripples have died away, you will see, on the surface of the water, a human face which will give sign to tell you your wish has been satisfied, always providing you have recited the magic words, which any

A very old bridge half hidden by greenery marks the entrance to the gorge of the Nahr al-Kalb.
(Photo Ch. Baugey.)

local boy will tell you.

The village of Smar Jbail has a very picturesque little *church* shaded by a huge oak-tree. It is consecrated to Mar Nohra, the saint who heals eye-diseases. This is a place of pilgrimage for eye-sufferers.

A few kilometres to the north of *Batroun* (old houses and outstanding lemonade), which was a large coastal village (Botrys) in antiquity, you can go by a narrow road which follows the Nahr el-Jaouz to the impressive ruins of the *castle of Mseilha* — a wild stronghold which might have come out of a sketch by Victor Hugo (3 kilometres from the coast).

Itinerary: 50 km from Beirut. 11 km north of Jbail, take a road to the right (it is not sign-posted, so you must ask) and follow it for 3 km. Turn left opposite the abstract sculpture by the side of the road.
Smar Jbail is 2.5 km further along the same road.

Accommodation: Jbail, 1 hotel*** and 2 hotels**.

■ If the visitor to Saida, full of classical and Biblical memories, imagines that he is about to plunge into the purple splendour of antiquity, he may be somewhat disappointed. What is there here to remind us of the mixing bowl offered by Achilles in the "Iliad" as a prize for a race ("a tooled silver mixing bowl containing six measures, but one which was finer than all others chiefly on account of its beauty. It had been beautifully engraved by the skilful Sidonians...")? What is there to recall the proud declaration in the "Odyssey" of the Sidonian woman who enticed away Eumaeus, the swineherd of Ulysses ("But I am from Sidon, the great bronze market"), the now nostalgic mention by Strabo of "Sidonian women skilled in embroidering veils" and the "fine houses of which Ulysses spoke"?
At Saida itself there remains nothing

Since the Crusades, the site of Saida has been dominated by the Sea Castle where Saint Louis stayed.
(Photo Marinier.)

of the glory that was Sidon. Nothing except a hill 40 metres high and 100 metres long, composed of a heap of murex shells — bearing witness to the extent of the purple-dye industry — that dye of antiquity which was so famous that its colour was a symbol of glory and supreme power among the Romans.

Gérard de Nerval, who stayed at the khan Frange at Saida in 1843, made up for his disappointment with philosophical considerations in his "Voyage en Orient": "Six leagues further on is Saida, the former Sidon, with its white houses clustering like a flock of sheep round the foothills of the mountains inhabited by the Druzes. These renowned shores have few ruins to show as memories of rich Phoenicia, but what can be left by towns where nothing but trade flourished? Their splendour has passed away like dust, and the curse of the Biblical books has been utterly fulfilled, just as everything which the poets dream and everything denied by the wisdom of nations!". But this is like looking for the dead among the living.

Saida today is a live town — very much alive. The visitor soon realizes this as he walks through the teeming streets of this capital and market of southern Lebanon. Its traditional activity as a provincial city takes on international dimensions 8 kilometres to the south with the refineries of Zahrani, the terminal of Tapline which brings the oil of Saudi Arabia to the Mediterranean.

The destiny of Saida was inherent in its geographical position. The small rocky promontory and range of islands upon which the town was built gave it a strategic position and provided excellent moorings. Moreover, Saida is at the centre of a long,

Segments of ancient columns of hard stone were used for reinforcing the limestone blocks of buildings erected by the Crusaders.
(Photo Marinier.)

rich plain 13 kilometres in length which has excellent water supplies. Enormously wealthy estates hidden from the gaze of the curious and protected from marauders by high walls, fences or screens of trees enclose Saida in a vast wall of orchards.

The neighbouring mountain to the east no longer has the deep valleys and steep slopes which, to the north, made the crossing of it difficult. It therefore provided comparatively easy access for the caravans coming from or going to Jezzine, Machgara and the Bekaa. Saint Paul followed this route, and the "road to Damascus" begins at Saida.

Sidon and the Crusaders

But although the vestiges of the Phoenician glory of Sidon are buried under the present-day city, Saida is rich in souvenirs of the Middle Ages. Its *"sea castle"* *(Qalaat el Bahr)* built on an islet connected to the mainland by a dike, is a beauty in itself.

Once you have forgotten the Crusaders and Saint Louis, this fortress arouses the profound pleasure offered by secular buildings rising against the eternity of the sea, to which they are exactly attuned. The patina on these old ochre-coloured, brown and reddish stones pierced by the cold blue disks of granite of the sawn off columns introduced horizontally into the structure of the walls has something magic about it. This motionless mass on the deep blue of the sea is a call to travel and dreams. The "sea castle" does not call to mind adjectives connected with the formidable, the powerful, the impregnable nor even the mysterious or strange, but rather with the pleasant, the prepossessing and even the pretty. Saida enjoys the luxury of a wonderful marine setting. However, inside the "sea castle", under the dark vaults of some of the halls and in the courtyard scattered with rusty bombards, column tambours and cut stones, the past lives again — intensely.

The harbour

And the visitor who looks out to the west of the harbour, where fishing boats and yachts jostle one another in front of the houses of the old town, finds himself back again in old Sidon, for this was one of the harbours of antiquity. From here went forth the Phoenician ships carrying Phoenician merchandise as far as the misty seas, exploring unknown lands, and fighting for Baal or Melqart or in the service of the master or ally of the moment, Egypt, Persia or Greece, until the curse of Ezekiel was fulfilled:

"For I will send into her pestilence; and blood into her streets; and the wounded shall be judged in the midst of her by the sword upon her on every side..."

The "Sea Castle"

The "sea castle" was built by the Crusaders during the winter of 1227 to 1228. These men, who were awaiting the arrival of Frederick II, left Akka to fortify the harbour of Sidon. The operation was conducted expeditiously. In three or four months, the elements of the edifice were in place: a large and a medium-sized tower connected by a curtain. Today, the "sea castle" has lost its original large tower — the one on the left — and only the foundations of it remain. What can be seen is the work of the Arabs, after the Crusaders had abandoned the fortress in 1291. The rectangular tower — on the right — is definitely Frankish. It is here that we can see how ancient columns were shamelessly used to reinforce the walls.

Just as the "sea castle" inspires us with joy and exaltation, so the *"land* castle" or "castle of Saint Louis", which is on a hill in the old town 200 metres north of the murex-shell hill, inspires sadness. According to Paul-Henri Eydoux, author of "Châteaux fantastiques", it was not the "castle of Saint Louis" that the French king occupied during his lengthy stays in the capital of the Seigneurie of Sagette, but the "sea castle", where he finds evidence of a royal residence in certain features of the decoration.

Between the "sea castle" and the "land castle" stretches the old town with its high narrow, winding souks where the smell of grilled meat and spices mingles with that of sawdust. Curiosity seekers will find here objects of delight, such as donkey collars woven from purple wool and decorated with sea shells and bluish-green rings.

The "khan Frange", a haven of refuge, and flowers built by Emir Fakhreddin, received French dealers and travellers from the seventeenth to the nineteenth centuries. The French consul in Saida lived there. The vaulted galleries of the ground floor were used as warehouses, while the first floor, also vaulted, was used for accomodation. The break between the silence and freshness of this place, together with its courtyard and central pool, and the agitated noise and tumult of the souks is most striking. Further south, almost on the seashore, the grand mosque which was formerly the church of the hospital of St John, rises like a fortress.

Next door to the "sea castle", the Rest-House of the National Tourist Council, with its vast lawn dominated by a huge white abstract sculpture, makes a sharp contrast with the fortress and combines modernism and tradition for the greater comfort of the traveller. The restaurant and seashore terrace are very agreeable. It looks like an Arab palace with almost windowless outside walls, though inside there are a fine patio with a fountain, and shady corridors in the walls of which old Arab ceramics have been placed.

The temple of Echmoun

A visit to Saida would not be complete without the ruins of the temple of Echmoun 4 kilometres north-east of the town. This was a Phoenician temple dedicated to Echmoun, the God of healing, to whom an entire dynasty of Sidonese kings appear to have devoted a special cult. This somewhat mysterious god recalls Aesculapius and Adonis, and, like the latter, incarnated the myth of rebirth. The terraced temple with its reddish stones, built on a magnificent site, although the only Phoenician temple which is well preserved, today provides the visitor with only a very confused impression. This chaotic work site, where large-scale excavation is still proceeding, will soon, no doubt, be organized into a clearer and more legible pattern. The present-day visitor can only admire fragments — a stone throne, a bas-relief, a Byzantine mosaic — and muse before the thick wall backing the esplanade on the interior by which the famous Phoenician inscriptions, discovered in 1900 and today scattered throughout the museums of the world, were hidden.

Name: transcription of the Phoenician name Saidoun (Sidon), from "said" (hunting). Echmoun: Phoenician name.

Sea Castle open from 8.30 a.m. to 12.30 and 2 p.m. to sundown. Admission free. Echmoun: Open from 8.30 a.m. to 12.30 and from 2 p.m. to sundown. Admission free.

Itinerary: 43 km from Beirut on Tyre (Sour) road.

Accommodation: 4 hotels* A restaurant, the «Rest House», on the sea shore to the North of the town.

Camping: Sarepta and Kasr el-Bahr, at Sarafand (10 km to the South, on the beach).

■

MAASSER ECH-CHOUF, see Chouf and Jezzine.
MOUKHTARA, see Chouf.
MSEILHA, see Rachana.

sir ed-danniye

■ A Virgilian landscape in a Dantesque framework in the north of Lebanon. You are surrounded by apple, apricot and peach-trees in lovingly kept orchards. Everywhere gushing springs can be heard, and sometimes the water, led through a precarious channel, crosses the road to go and irrigate a thirsty field or orchard on the other side. Nowhere does the surrounding mountain allow the slightest bare rock to appear. There is nothing but greenery, though it covers the savage slopes of the escarpments of valleys with steep sides and deep gorges.

The contrast between this wild mountain structure and the pleasant profusion of the orchards is disconcerting.

The Far-West of Lebanon

Nestling in this cool, very cool verdure, the small town of Sir ed-Danniye, the chief inhabited place of the area, stands out on an impressive escarpment. The vast, flowery garden of the chief hotel provides an admirable view. This township is just silence and rest. It even appears to be empty. The cafés and restaurants with their fine shaded terraces are asleep.

The impression of wealth conveyed by the orchards is a fallacious one, for the fruit, and above all the apples, now bring little profit. And yet, it would be difficult to find a place which is healthier or cooler in summer than this town lost in the greenery. There are week-end houses at Sir ed-Danniye. It is a place for summer holidays, but not very fashionable, and not much frequented, which is a pity.

The temples of Sfire

From Sir ed-Danniye, by following a road which, at each of its vertiginous curves, reveals another magnificent panorama, you arrive at the village of *Sfire*. The road gets gradually worse, and the landscape progressively wilder.

Sfire itself, which can be reached by car, gives the impression of being the end of the world. At the end of the village, donkeys are waiting to transport to Tripoli goatskins full of curdled milk. Half a dozen of these bloated containers, with a few hairs still attached to them, are lying on the ground. In the mud created by a spring which gushes forth near this "dairy", the women are filling the skins and tying up the opening, while the men load them onto the donkeys.

After a few hundred yards' climbing, you find the ruins of the *two Roman temples* of Sfire, almost backing onto the bare mountain and dominating the surroundings like a castle. This position, and the fact that one of the temples is preserved up to and including the roof, make Sfire one of the most interesting archaeological curiosities of Lebanon, next to the great and famous ruins.

Name: Sir ed-Danniye or Sir.	
Altitude: 950 m. Sfire: 1,300 m.	
Itinerary: 31 km from Tripoli. Sfire, 7 km from Sir.	
Accommodation: 3 hotels** and 6 hotels*.	

■
NABI YACOUB, see Chouf.
NAHR AL-LABAN, (natural bridge), see Fakra.

NAHR IBRAHIM, see Afqa.
NIHA (temples of), see Zahle.
NIHA OF CHOUF, see Chouf.

sour (tyre)

■ In the warm light of the setting sun, with sails unfurled or motors humming, the fishing-boats of Tyre combine their efforts to pull in their heavy nets. The fishermen, panting with the strain, accompany the movement of their muscular brown arms with a strange chant of three syllables, the first low and drawn out, the second low too but somewhat shorter, and the third sharp and sudden like the grunt of a woodcutter. These three rhythmic syllables are: "E-li-ssa!"

Elissa

And there we have 2,850 years of particularly turbulent history done away with at one go. Elissa was the princess of Tyre who was obliged by the tyranny of her brother Pygmalion to flee into exile and who, at the head of a handful of Tyrian émigrés, founded Carthage (from the Phoenician *Qart Hadasht* — or new town) about 815 B.C. — she to whom the Greeks and Romans gave the name Dido (the fugitive).

The fact that poor fishermen still encourage themselves today by chanting the three syllables of the name of that illustrious daughter of a king of Tyre, the proud queen of the seas, is sufficient to transfigure this poor township (36,000 inhabitants, they say, but the figure is probably exaggerated), the past grandeur of which still feeds nostalgia of minds full of the sound of legends.

"What city is like Tyrus, in the midst of the sea? When thy wares went forth out of the seas, thou filledst many peoples; thou didst enrich the kings of the earth with the multitude of thy riches and of thy merchandise."

Thus, the grim prophet Ezekiel, vaticinating during the sixth century B.C., mingled with his vision of the downfall of Tyre a description of its grandeur.

the temple of Melqart

The present-day port of Sour, which occupies a part of the former site of the ancient northern one (the southern, or Egyptian one having been abandoned since the Byzantine epoch), is very modest, but also very pretty.

After looking at the excavations, the visitor can come and meditate here on the grandeur of the past in a café-restaurant-hotel which is quite pleasant but too sophisticated for this place. From here the visitor to Tyre can contemplate peacefully and unhurriedly the little fishing-port, the tiny, busy old town crowded up at the end of what was formerly a string of islands, the long narrow strip of land joining it to the mainland 600 metres away, and the coast with its valleys and mountains fading away into a bluish mist to the north.

The islets which formed ancient Tyre have been welded together during the course of the centuries, the last having been linked up during the reign of the second king of the city, the famous Hiram (whose tomb is, probably erroneously, supposed to be a Phoenician funereal monument which can be seen 6 kilometres from the town on the right of the Kana road), a contemporary of David and Solomon (tenth century B.C.).

Hiram had built a temple to the God of his town, Melqart (from *Melek* — king — and *Qart* — town), from which the ancients made the terrible Moloch to whom children were sacrificed (and, in fact, this sort of sacrifice continued till the fourth century). A temple, the dimensions and richness of which were in line with the importance of the enlarged city.

Two steles, one of gold and consecrated to fire and the other of emerald consecrated to the wind, stood on each side of the entrance to the magnificent edifice, the renown of which confirmed Hiram's reputation as a builder to such an extent that King David consulted the sovereign of Tyre regarding the building of a temple to his God, Jehovah, in his capital.

Solomon, the son of David, made this dream a reality thanks to the assistance of Hiram, who sent him his architect, foundrymen and goldsmiths and provided the materials (gold, bronze and cedar wood) with which to build the famous temple of Solomon, to a large extent inspired by the temple of Melqart.

Nothing remains of the temple of Melqart, but the fishermen of Tyre and enthusiastic amateur archaeologists still hope to find, one day, at the bottom of the sea, the fabulous columns of gold and emerald.

The great task of the archaeologists

Since 1947, the past of Tyre has been rising from the sea and the sand. Excavations have been undertaken on a gigantic scale. These are still continuing under the direction of the Emir Maurice Chehab, Director General of Antiquities (his monograph "Tyre" constitutes the most valuable guide for a fruitful tour of this complex site). This is an arduous task, for vestiges of the civilizations of the Phoenicians, the Greco-Romans, the Byzantines, the Arabs and the Crusaders, each of whom shamelessly destroyed the buildings of their predecessors in order to use their materials, are superimposed on one another.

At the roundabout at the entrance to the town, very clear sign-posts lead the visitor to three huge excavation sites (each of which extends over more than 12 acres), which can be reached by car.

(1) Metropolis excavations

A fine Byzantine road of limestone slabs about 500 metres long, lined with tombs containing very richly sculptured Roman sarcophagi (though the best have been taken to the Beirut Museum) leads to a *monumental arch* and slightly beyond, where it drops about 50 centimetres so as to reveal the paved Roman road which it covered. The arch, which dates from the end of the second century, must have fallen down during an earthquake in the sixth century. It has been put up again, and the central part rises to a height of some 20 metres. The remains of a large *aqueduct*, the internal structure of which is well preserved to a distance of about 300 metres from the arch, runs alongside the Byzantine road.

This excavation site also reveals considerable Byzantine remains — a curious *necropolis* which incorporated a garden as if for the living, a tomb decorated with frescoes, funeral enclosures, a funeral chapel, fragments of mosaics, and baths.

Recent excavations near the necropolis have revealed one of the largest (and best preserved) Roman *hippodromes* in the world. Under the implacable summer sun, the impression the tourist has of this immense race-track, which appears to be extended to infinity by the sea at the end of it, is one of the most utterly nostalgic it is possible to experience. Standing under the arcades of the covered walks and tiers of the amphitheatre, partially reconstituted, you expect, and hope for with ridiculously bated breath, the noise of the mingled crowd of people from Mount Lebanon and their Roman masters.

(2) City excavations

Two kilometres further on, the *remains of the city* have been revealed. In the centre, a broad avenue advances majestically towards the sea, triumphantly protected by columns of veined marble. The last

The ruins of Tyre are the most extensive in Lebanon; they cover more than 40 acres.
(Photo NCT.)

(Byzantine) paving of white marble was laid over another, fourth century, paving consisting exclusively of mosaic, some of which has been disclosed.

The melancholy, grandiose ensemble appears chaotic to the lay visitor who, apart from this avenue and its colonnades, has the impression of walking over a basement. But it is a basement which the archaeologists are bringing back to life, revealing here an arena, there a palestra, water-tanks and the houses of a residential quarter, thermal baths the remarkably designed fittings of which still appear quite clearly, and the blurred vestiges of the walls of the Crusaders' castle.

(3) The cathedral excavation

These are the excavations which have made least progress. Separated from those of the city only by the existing road, they are due to be extended as far as the sea. The *cathedral* now in ruins was built by the Crusaders according to the traditional plan of Romanesque churches of the twelfth century.

The enormous monolithic columns of pink Aswan granite indicate that the builders took their materials from some neighbouring Roman building which has now disappeared. The church itself was built 2.5 metres above a Roman road. The cathedral of Tyre is not very thrilling in itself, but when you realize that, during the thirteenth century, the Kings of Jerusalem came to be crowned there (for a purely symbolic monarchy, by the way) and that the corpse of the German Emperor Frederick Barbarossa was placed there, waiting in vain to be taken to the holy city, the greyish remains of this church provide food for the imagination.

The beaches of Sour

To come back to the present, the visitor to Tyre will find at the N.T.C. Rest-House, run by the Beirut Hotel Training School, a comfortable haven of rest. He can bathe on the hotel's own beach, not very crowded.

The town of Tyre has 7 kilometres of beach, and its present ambition is to become a major seaside resort.

Modern Tyre, which scarcely attracts any attention, would then be less overwhelmed by its fabulous past as the homeland of Europa daughter of Agenor, king of Tyre, whom Zeus, transformed into a seal, carried on his back to the continent to which she was to give her name, and of Cadmus, her brother, who invented the alphabet and went to teach it to the Greeks.

Name: Sour is an Arabic word meaning "rampart". The Hebrew word "Tsor" means rock.

Excavations open to visitors from 8.30 a.m. to 12.30 and from 2 p.m. to sundown. Admission free.

Itinerary: 85 km from Beirut.

Accommodation: Rest house and Beirut.

Camping: At Zour, near the «Rest House», and *Sarepta* and *Kasr el Bahr* at Sarafand (20 km North of Sour, on the beach).

■

QARAOUN (lake), see Bekaa.
QANOUAT AL-HERMEL (Pyramid of Hermel), see Hermel.
SIDON, see Saida.
SFIRE, see Sir ed-Danniye.
SMAR JBAIL, see Rachana.

Tyre, like Byblos, has an adorable little harbour where it is very pleasant to stroll.
(Photo Almasy.)

tripoli (trablous)

■ Whereas Beirut is disconcerting, Tripoli is satisfying. Coming from the airport, you penetrate into the city like a fly into a spider's web. Here, the town is in the country, and Tripoli receives you in the midst of its gardens.

There is a smooth urbanity about the way the city is planned. You pass almost unconsciously from the midst of orange-groves into urban traffic, and here too the roads are wide and their direction is clear. Everything leads to and from the huge roundabout of the *Place du Tell*, where there is a clock.

This, of course, is the modern part of the city, which extends without interruption from the old city to the harbour, the Mina. *El-Mina* is the name given to the oldest part of Tripoli, the place where, about 2,700 years ago, was built the Phoenician town of which nothing remains today.

The triple town

Today, Tripoli is the second city of Lebanon (population over 150,000). It is the capital of the north, a fairly homogeneous city with a predominantly Sunnite Moslem population, which is more typical of Lebanon than Beirut. In a way it constitutes a balancing factor which compensates to some extent for the monstrous development of the Lebanese capital. Tripoli (the Arabic name Trablous is merely a corruption of the Greek), the triple town, owes its name primarily to history but also to geography. The three great Phoenician cities — Tyre (Sour), Sidon (Saida) and Aradus (Arwad in Syria) set up a confederation at El-Mina, which was then a rocky island whose situation at the mouth of a natural depression later to be known as the Homs-Tripoli depression, the trading and invasion route near the mouth of the Kadisha river (holy valley) and perfectly suited the plans of the enterprising city-states. Tyrians, Sidonians and Aradians, each had their separate districts there.

This, then, was a triple town and remained so even when the alluvium from the Nahr el Awali (modern name of the little river which runs through Tripoli and is known as the Nahr Kadisha for the first part of its course) united El-Mina to the mainland.

Tripoli still is triple, for the old town consists of two distinct hills separated by the Nahr el-Awali, whose cemented bed gives it the mournful aspect of a canal. The visitor is amazed when told that this is the "fountain of the gardens" of the Song of Songs. On the other hand, others say that the "fountain of the gardens" was the Orontes.

The modern town extends to the west from the foot of the hill on the left bank. Tripoli proper is 2 kilometres from El-Mina.

The old town

This very prepossessing new town is, however, of only limited interest to the tourist, who, once he has tried the famous Tripolitanian pastries such as *znout esset* (ladies' arms) and *echta* (cream), will want to visit the old town on the left bank of the Nahr el-Awali, dominated by the *citadel*, the *castle of Saint-Gilles (Qalaat Sanjil)* around which the mediaeval city was built. This remarkably well preserved mediaeval city will make upon him an irresistible impression of the permanence of the past.

The past is also there on the other hill opposite *(Qoubbe)* where the gaudy-coloured houses, a heterogeneous assembly of ancient and modern, sordid and comfortable, stick out on the forward edge of a steep slope. At the foot of the castle, the labyrinth of souks, madrasahs (schools of religious science), mosques and khans (caravanserais or warehouses) have

At Tripoli, the al-Khayattine market, with its elegant arcatures open to the sky, brings the visitor back to a scene of the fourteenth century.
(Photo Marinier.)

retained the form they had at the time of the Mamelukes.

Souks and mosques

The souks of Tripoli are the finest in Lebanon. One of them, which surpasses all others in architectural and human interest, is the *souk el-Khayattine* (tailors' market), with its splayed arches silhouetted against the blue sky and the craftsmen, each installed in his odd little niche, seated on a sort of low table and sewing by hand, while others work the treadle of their sewing-machines in the open air. This is the same sort of work, apart from the machine, which has been going on for 600 years. The souks and khans perpetuate the time of the guilds.

There are also a *khan el-Misriyyine* (Egyptians' caravanserai) and a *khan el-Ashkar* (soldiers' caravanserai).

The *khan es-Saboun* (soap warehouse) has the beauty and peace of a cloister. A fountain, fed by a pool, plays in the shaded courtyard. Under the arcades of the first floor are stocked thousands of cubical cakes of green soap.

Near the Nahr el-Awali, the streets are given over to copper craftsmen, who can be seen hammering out humble utensils such as pots and pans, which will later be lined up in gloving lines on the shelves of the shop, or engraving ornamental trays. One activity of a more modern kind dominates — carpentry. Tripoli is the town of woodworking. Tripolitanian cabinet-makers have a great reputation, and the Lebanese come from afar to order their furniture there.

Apart from the madrasahs (of which there are about fifteen, the most famous being the *madrasah el-Saqraqiya* and the *madrasah el-Qartawiya)*, mosques and souks, the epoch of the Mamelukes survives in the form of several hammams (baths), such as the *hammam Ezz ed-Dine,* below the souks, near the Nahr el-A-wali,which has been in use since the fourteenth century. These hammams, which include both communal and private bath-rooms, have roofs in the form of cupolas with glass cabochons which provide lighting for the bath-rooms and corridors of the hammams.

Numerous mosques of the Mameluke epoch remain in Tripoli, and two of them are worthy of particular attention — the grand mosque with its fine square courtyard, all white with its low green domes, situated on the heights of the old town not far from the citadel, and the *mosque of Teylan* with its magnificent portal divided into alternate wide black and white stripes, situated on the way out of the town on the left of the road to Beirut.

The Citadel

The architecture of the *citadel*, which on one side dominates the mediaeval city by its enormous size (140 metres long and 70 metres wide) and on the other presents an impressive wall running down to the river, sums up a great deal of the history of Tripoli.

There remains but little of the most ancient evidence of the great buildings of the Crusaders. Raymond de Saint Gilles, Count of Toulouse, who in 1099 began the siege of Tripoli which lasted six years and was continued after Raymond's death in 1105 by his son Bertrand, undertook the construction of this fortress in 1102.

At first sight, the castle appears to be well preserved, but this is an illusion. Only the major part of the side overlooking the Nahr el-Awali, a few foundations and one wall of the chapel remain of the Crusaders' edifice. The Arabs set fire to the castle after taking it in 1289 and then rebuilt it. The new building was modified a number of times by the different governments which succeeded one another at Tripoli.

The citadel of Tripoli is, in fact, a real town with its shaded little narrow streets.

The Citadel did not only assume a defensive military rôle; it also constituted a collection of town dwellings, a barracks and a place of worship, though its defensive function remained predominant.

The result is that the visitor has the impression of wandering through a fortified town rather than a fortress — an impression which is sometimes strengthened by the sight of groups of men, women and children having a picnic beneath a fig-tree. He walks on over the vast esplanades, goes down narrow passages like gorges, and passes through huge vaulted halls flanked by disused stores. But the castle of the "distant Princess", of Melissande, princess of Tripoli, with whom the troubadour Jaufré Rudel fell in love without ever seeing her and who went to die in her arms, that castle is very dead.

The tower of Lions

After spending a long time wandering round the old town, the visitor will saunter through the *Mina*, where he will be struck with the number and size of the timber-yards of the port. The port itself is a very pleasant, though not very exotic, place for a walk, with its agreeable cafés and restaurants (excellent fish meals) from which can be seen the bare rocky islets frequented by Tripolitanian lovers of aquatic sports.

At the most desolate spot in the Mina, between the rail terminus with its desolate goods wagons and the sea, rises the best preserved example of Mameluke military architecture, the *tower of Lions (Borjes-Sba)*, a massive square tower with rounded corners. The lions with which it was decorated and which gave it its name have disappeared. This heavy, vigilant sentinel looked out over the sea and watched for Frankish and Genoese fleets.

The Tripoli of tomorrow

To the north of Tripoli, the twentieth century assails the visitor, with the huge refinery and the installations of the Beddawi terminal which receives Irakian oil by pipeline. But before he gets there, at *Qoubbet el-Beddawi* 3 kilometres from the town, a small *dervishery* flanked by a mosque and preceded by a garden of pine-trees with a café where men and women come to drink and smoke the narguileh, brings back to him the feeling of the permanence of the past. Behind the dervishery a wide, semi-circular pool fed by an abundant spring, always attracts a large number of sight-seers; it contains nacreous fishes, which may perhaps be a survival of a Phoenician superstition. As from the beginning of the Moslem conquest, Tripoli experienced an economic and cultural breakthrough. Its Arabic library contained more than 100,000 volumes when it went up in flames on the arrival of the Crusaders. Today, Tripoli still aspires to be a metropolis. Its thrust towards the future is symbolized by the extraordinary buildings put up for the *Tripoli International Fair*. This fair has been put off for nearly ten years, but the buildings for it in the midst of orange groves (the tracks leading to them are scarcely fit for cars and you have to ask your way), designed by Oscar Niemeyer, the famous architect of Brasilia, are already in place.

Name: from the Greek meaning "three towns". Trablous, the Arabic name, is a corruption of the Greek.

Qalaat Sanjil: open from 8.30 a.m. to 12.30 and from 2 p.m. to sundown. Mosques open every day except at times of prayer.

Itinerary: 83 km north of Beirut.

Accommodation: 1 hotel***, 2 hotels** and 21 hotels*.

■

TYRE, see Sour.

On the right bank of the Nahr al Awali, the houses of Qoubbe
are crowded into an amphitheatre.
(Photo NCT.)

zahle

zouk mkayel

■ Zahle, the capital of the Bekaa, is the town of *arak* and is embalmed in the sweetish, penetrating odour of that anisated drink. It is also the home of that Lebanese gastronomic speciality — the *mezzes*. It is a capital which stands aloof from its flat domain, clinging to the foothills of Mount Lebanon at the entrance to a valley well provided with water.

Zahle is a wealthy provincial town. It owes its prosperity to the vines which cover large areas of the Bekaa and from which is produced the anisated alcohol, *arak,* the most renowned brand of which is made here.

The town of mezzes

Water ripples at Zahle, and the entrance to the little valley is covered with an extraordinary series of huge open-air restaurants protected from the sun by awnings and numerous trees, where streams, fountains and lakes cool the air.

For nearly a kilometre we go straight from one restaurant to another. In any of them, the customer who orders a *mezze,* will find between thirty and forty different dishes laid out in front of him.

The temples of Niha

North-east of Zahle on the actual slopes of the Lebanon, the beautiful village of *Niha,* though scorched by the sun, courageously maintains its terraces owing to a lovely little watercourse which runs through them; it contains the ruins of a fine *Roman temple* dedicated to Hadaranes and of another little *sanctuary,* both of them so well in tune with the bare slopes surrounding them they seem to have been born of them. If you have the courage to walk 3 kilometres northward, you will discover, in much wilder surroundings, *two other Roman temples,* those of Hosn Niha.

■ If we leave the Tripoli motorway after crossing the Nahr al-Kalb but before arriving at the Bay of Jounie and start climbing the hills which run down to the sea, we immediately run through a village which already exudes the serenity of mountain communities.

A number of small workshops line the main road. They consist each of a single cool room where the electric light is on all day, though in some cases there is a narrow window which gives a meagre light and the double doors are thrown open to admit more. These are the workshops of the weavers.

Further on, to the right, there is a bigger, modern, four-square building, with plenty of lighting and a fine interior courtyard. This is a weaving centre of the Ministry of Industry, with well-lighted, yet cool workshops.

Both the publicly and privately owned workshops of Zouk Mkayel weave silk, satin, wool, and luxury fabrics and gold and silver brocades of an Oriental character. With these traditional fabrics they also make very fine clothing such as caftans and abayas, and table linen, table-cloths, napkins and table runners. But they also weave naïve effigies of saints and decorative materials imitating the works of non-figurative painters.

Elegant women from Beirut and abroad who come to rummage among these sumptuous clothes and try them on with obvious pleasure, say that these garments, some of which are of breath-taking beauty, cost half what they would in specialized shops in the Lebanese capital.

A dying craft

For some years, Zouk Mkayel has been half asleep. The movements of the weavers are anything but those of the busy bee. To be sure, the shuttle still slides neatly through the ''shed'' like a furtive animal, but the entire activity gives an impression of disillusionment, except in the case of the precious gold and silver brocades on silk, where the delicacy of the work, and the thinness of the silk threads require an extreme attention from both men and women workers. These devoted craftsmen do not even raise their eyes from their work to reply to the few interested tourists who put questions to them about their work. Most of the other weavers just hang about idly. Many looms are unoccupied, and the boss himself sits down at one to give a demonstration to visitors.

The fact is that the prosperity of this luxury craft mainly depends on tourists.

However that may be, it is still possible to discover, at the very gates of Beirut (and even inside Beirut), small communities which have maintained a certain mountain-dweller's authenticity and still have conscientious craftsmen proud of their methods and products.

Name: means "Michael's farm".

Itinerary: 17 km from Beirut on the Tripoli road; fork between the Nahr al-Kalb and (sign-posted).

Accommodation: Beirut.

ZAHLE (see note page 164).

Altitude: 960 m. Temples of Niha, 1,000 m.

Itinerary: 54 km from Beirut. 10 km from Chtaura, to the left on the Baalbek road. Niha, 11 km from Zahle. Take the left-hand road at the fork before arriving at Ablah, then the second to the left; thence 1.7 km to Niha.

Accommodation: 1 hotel***, 1 hotel** and 12 hotels*.

■

ZAHRANI, see Saida.

Weaving is carried out at Zouk Mkayel, but also in many other parts of Lebanon, particularly the Chouf area.
(Photo NCT.)

lebanese
journey

maps of lebanon

The limited size of the country and the fact that the two railway lines (Tripoli-Beirut-Naqoura and Beirut-Damascus) are now exclusively reserved for goods traffic, leave the visitor with no choice but to travel by road.

By using buses, he will gain an insight into the picturesque human side of the country and make a considerable saving — it only costs one Lebanese pound to go by bus from Beirut to Tripoli or Sour (Tyre) or to any intermediate stop, incidentally.

But the traveller who wants to be independent must use a car — private car, hired car (with or without driver) or taxi.

It is therefore essential to be well provided with reliable maps, and we may as well say straight away that there are no up-to-date reliable road-maps of Lebanon. Moreover, the sign-posting (usually in Arabic and Roman characters) leaves something to be desired as soon as you get off the beaten track (which is precisely what the present work seeks to encourage the visitor to do), where all you find is a few sign-posts in Arabic only or none at all.

The bookshops in Beirut (the best stocked is the *Librairie Antoïne* at Hamra and Bab Edriss) sell:

—a Shell 1:200,000 folding road-map which is notoriously inadequate;

—a large road and tourist map consisting of a single sheet (104 × 75 cm) which has to be rolled up and cannot be used in a car; it is quite good but must have been established around 1965-1966, and therefore shows as tracks certain roads which today are excellent asphalted roads;

—a 1: 100,000 map in 21 folding sheets; this is the best and has been sold since the summer of 1973 in a new cover with the Shell emblem printed on it; however, since it is merely a reproduction of the map published by the Department of

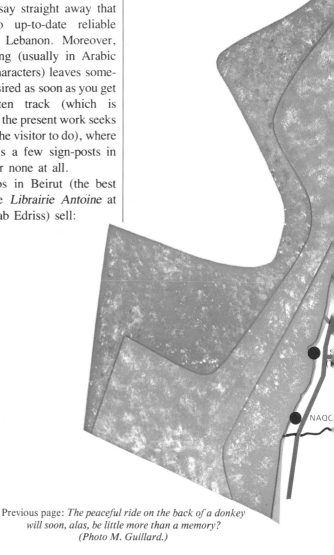

NAQOU

Previous page: The peaceful ride on the back of a donkey will soon, alas, be little more than a memory?
(Photo M. Guillard.)

Major natural and tourist regions.

Geographical Affairs in 1965, it is not up-to-date.

Another disadvantage of these last two maps is a lack of clarity and the fact that the distances between localities are practically illegible (and not marked at all in the case of some stretches of road), while the legend is most incomplete.

As for the "Tourist Map of Lebanon" at a scale of 1: 200,000 which is usually offered to the tourist, the least said the better, except that it is so confused it is quite unusable by the motorist, though it does give an idea of the extraordinary archaeological heritage of Lebanon.

Certain Arabic words which occur frequently on the maps are worthy of translation: *ras*, cape; *deir*, convent; *beit*, house; *nahr*, river; *wadi*, watercourse; *jabal*, mountain; *ain*, source; *nabeh*, source; *ard*, land; *borj*, tower; *bab*, gate; *arz*, cedars; *el faouqa*, height; *el tahta*, bottom; *kfar*, fortress; *ksar*, palace; *qalaat*, castle; *nabi*, prophet; *mar*, saint; *tell*, plain...

In Lebanon place-names are either of Arabic or of Phoenician origin, but the only official transcription is into Arabic script. Transcription into Roman characters involves the use of many ways of spelling owing to the fact that the majority of vowels in Arabic have no exact equivalent in European languages, that certain phonemes do not exist in either and that words differ slightly according as they are transcribed for English or French-speaking people. But the visitor who exercises a certain amount of mental agility will have little difficulty.

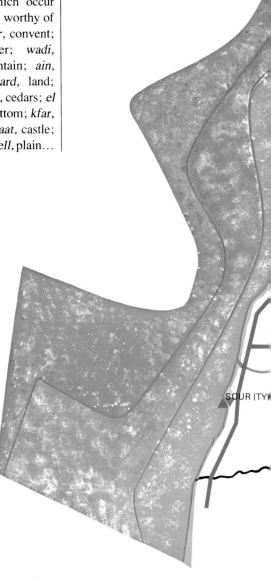

SOUR (TY

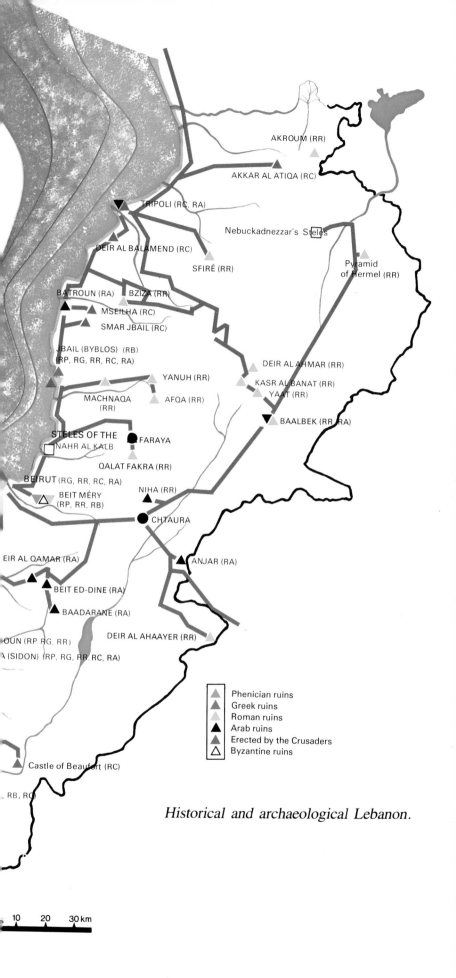

AKROUM (RR)

AKKAR AL ATIQA (RC)

TRIPOLI (RC, RA)

Nebuckadnezzar's Steles

DEIR AL BALAMEND (RC)

SFIRÉ (RR)

Pyramid
of Hermel (RR)

BATROUN (RA)   BZIZA (RR)

MSEILHA (RC)

SMAR JBAIL (RC)

JBAIL (BYBLOS) (RB)
(RP, RG, RR, RC, RA)

DEIR AL AHMAR (RR)

YANUH (RR)

KASR AL BANAT (RR)
YAAT (RR)

MACHNAQA   AFQA (RR)
(RR)

BAALBEK (RR, RA)

STELES OF THE   FARAYA
NAHR AL KALB

QALAT FAKRA (RR)

BEIRUT (RG, RR, RC, RA)

BEIT MÉRY   NIHA (RR)
(RP, RR, RB)

CHTAURA

EIR AL QAMAR (RA)

ANJAR (RA)

BEIT ED-DINE (RA)

BAADARANE (RA)

DEIR AL AHAAYER (RR)

OUN (RP RG, RR)

A (SIDON) (RP, RG, RR, RC, RA)

Phenician ruins
Greek ruins
Roman ruins
Arab ruins
Erected by the Crusaders
Byzantine ruins

Castle of Beaufort (RC)

, RB, RC)

Historical and archaeological Lebanon.

10   20   30 km

how to get to lebanon

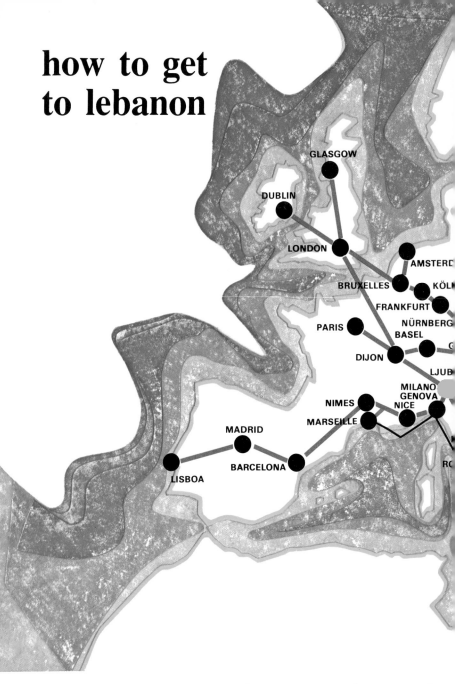

By air

The majority of visitors to Lebanon go by air. The International Airport of Beirut, situated at Khalde, 7 km from the capital, is the most modern and best equipped in the Middle East and is used by most leading air-lines — PANAM, BOAC, Air-France, KLM, Lufthansa, Sabena, Swissair, Alitalia, Air India, JAL, Aeroflot... and by the air-lines of the Arab countries — SAA (Saudi Arabia), Egyptair, Gulf Aviation (Federation of Arabian Emirates), Lybian Arab Air Lines, etc...

In 1972, 37 companies were operating regular services through Beirut International Airport and 52 others used it for non-regular traffic.

The Lebanese Company, Middle East Air Lines (MEA), whose traffic far predominates, operates to London, Copenhagen, Brussels, Paris, Nice, Frankfort, Zurich, Geneva, Vienna, Milan, Rome, Athens, Benghazi, Bagdad, Kuwait, Teheran, Jeddah, Dhahran, Bahrein, Aden, Doha, Abu Dhabi, Dubai, Muskat, Khartum, Kano, Lagos, Accra, Abidjan, Robertsfield, Freetown, Sofia, Budapest,

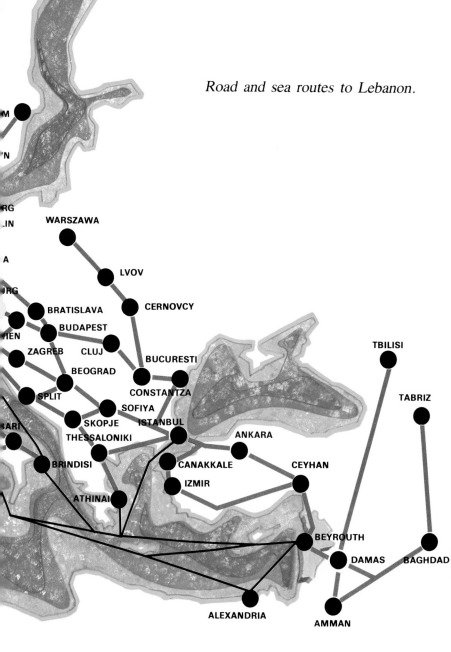

Road and sea routes to Lebanon.

Warsaw, Berlin, Ankara, Istanbul, Nicosia, Cairo and Amman.

It has agencies in all the chief towns of the world and works in a pool with the leading companies, applying the international tariff system ("F", first class, "Y", economy class, "YE" economy class with 35 % reduction on return fares for tickets valid from 10 to 30 days).

By Sea

You can go to Lebanon by sea, and the two shipping companies which call regularly at Beirut call at numerous other ports, thus enabling the visitor to complete his holiday with a Mediterranean cruise and disembark with his car either at Istanbul or at Izmir. The traveller can use the Turkish shipping lines (Denizcilik Bankasi) or the Italian Adriatica shipping company.

The Turkish lines make a regular circuit calling at Beirut alternately from the south and the north — Istanbul, Izmir, the Piraeus, Naples, Marseilles, Barcelona, Marseilles, Genoa, Naples, Alexandria, Beirut, Alexandria, Naples, Marseilles, Barcelona, Genoa, Naples, the Piraeus,

Istanbul. There are two to three weeks' intervals between departures. The Adriatica lines call at Trieste, Venice, Genoa, Marseilles, Brindisi, Naples, Alexandria, Rhodes, Beirut, Famagusta (Cyprus), Adalia, Heraklion (Crete), Nauplia, Katakolon, Izmir, Syracuse, Dubrovnik and Bari.

By road

Getting to Lebanon by road presents no difficulty. For example, the journey from Paris to Beirut can be done in from five to eight days via Italy, Yugoslavia, Bulgaria, Greece, Turkey and Syria.

Beirut.

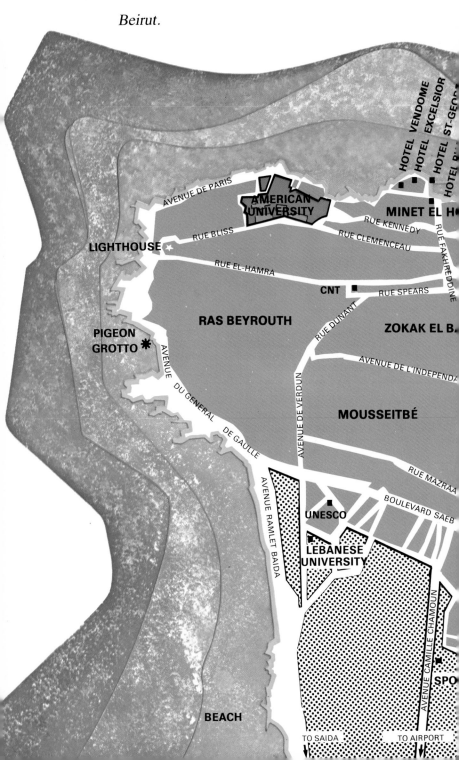

The majority of the route consists of motorways. The European motorway E 5, which is an extension from Calais of the British motorway E 2 from London, takes the motorist as far as the Turko-Syrian frontier through Brussels, Liège, Frankfort, Nuremberg, Vienna, Budapest, Belgrade, Sofia, Istanbul, Ankara, Adana and Anakya. He then has a good road before him via Latakia to Beirut.

All roads leading to Istanbul, and there are many of them, will do. For the Middle East, Damascus is still the nodal point for all roads leading to Lebanon.

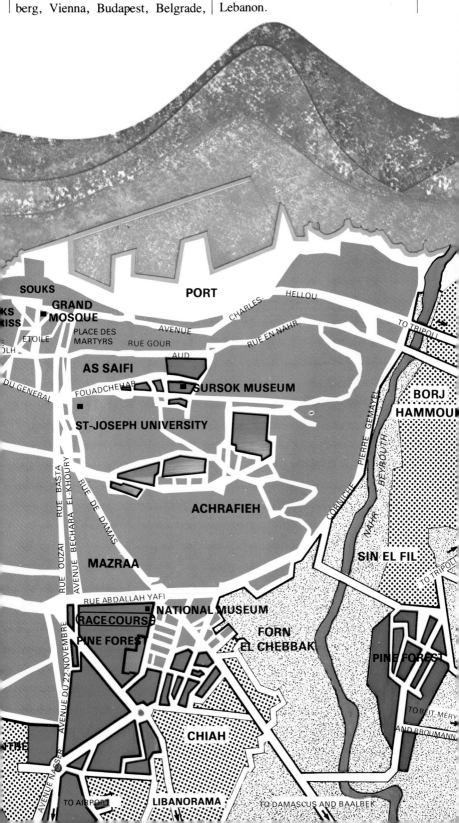

driving in lebanon

The motorist driving in Lebanon for the first time is terrified by the standard of driving there. The Highway Code is completely ignored. The result is that the new-comer to the roads of Lebanon must make up his mind that anything can happen at any moment. And it is because he is convinced of this that the Lebanese driver gives evidence of a diabolical virtuosity and an imperturbable calm. There is no priority; crossing over continuous white lines and passing on blind corners are the usual thing; full head-lights are frequently used instead of dipped lights; ignoring traffic lights is, in fact, tolerated as soon as traffic in the cities becomes less dense... However, it is a remarkable fact that there are not many accidents, in spite of the innumerable narrow and sinuous mountain roads. There is no speed-limit except where such is indicated by sign-boards, but the roads do not allow of excessive speed. The visiting motorist, therefore, should not get exited but exercise constant vigilance and, above all, never drive in accordance with what would be a supremely dangerous principle — ''I am in the right, so I can go ahead.''

You have to be at least 21 years of age to drive a car in Lebanon.

Car Hire

There are numerous companies which hire cars with or without chauffeur, the chief ones being Hertz, Avis, Integra and Lenacar. Reservations are usually made through the representatives of these agencies in foreign countries. It should be remembered that these cars cannot be taken outside the country where they are hired.

Petrol

Petrol is cheap and there are plenty of petrol stations, which are often only about two or three hundred metres apart on busy roads.

Insurance

Insurance is not compulsory but is, of course, highly recommended. The green international insurance certificate is valid. You must, of course, have an international driving licence, and for a stay of more than three months a tryptique is required.

Breakdowns

Breakdowns are no problem. All the leading car manufacturers have their agents here, though their workshops take perhaps a bit longer to carry out repairs. The motorist will find numerous garages staffed by very capable and competent mechanics. In any case, as soon as a car breaks down in Lebanon, all other motorists stop to give assistance to the unfortunate driver.

Lastly, the Automobile and Touring Club of Lebanon (ATCL) provides information and advice to members of foreign clubs (Telephone 22.92.22, 22.16.98 and 22.16.99) and can, in particular, validitate the national driving licence if this is not valid as an international one.

Taxi

However, for day trips, the visitor can always use taxis, which are very numerous. These can only be distinguished from private cars by the colour of their number plates, which are red. They have no taximeters; most of them are Mercedes.

As in the towns, there are two sorts of taxis — ordinary ones and ''service taxis''. They look exactly the same, but after having hailed the taxi, you ask ''Service?'' (the French word used in Arabic) to find out. The ''service taxis'' take up to five passengers either from their stand or as ''pick-ups'' and drop them on their route; they charge very low fares — 25 LP in town, or 50 LP for about ten kilometres, LL 1 for twenty kilometres, etc. (slight extra charge on Sundays). The ordinary taxi will ask LL 5 to take you to Beit Mery, Broummana or Nahr al-Kalb, and LL 10 to 12 for Jbail. The fare is often the subject of haggling. This is the case with the taxis whose stand is at the *Place des Martyrs* in Beirut, which is the point of arrival from and departure to all directions. The others, which are more expensive (though here again, haggling is the order of the day), have their permanent stand in front of the major hotels, particularly the *Saint Georges.*

The visitor who wishes to avoid this disadvantage or who cares nothing for local customs (the departure of taxis and buses from the Place des Martyrs is a spectacle in itself) can always telephone to one of the big companies, such as Lebanon Taxis or National Taxis, which will send him an American battleship gleaming with chrome and tell him what his journey will cost, without haggling. He should also know that taxis wait for their customers for a very modest fee. Thus, he can drive from Beirut to the Lebanese Casino at Maamelteine (25 km), stay there for three or four hours and come back to Beirut for about LL 30.

THE ROADS OF LEBANON

(According to the statistics of the Ministry of Public Works in 1973)

International roads	570 km
Main roads	1,420 km
Local secondary roads	4,410 km
Inland roads (in the towns and villages)	700 km
Total	7,100 km

The Tripoli motorway does not as yet go any further than Maamelteine (25 km from Beirut). Towards the south, there is the commencement of a motorway as far as Khalde (7 km) and the road to Damascus is, on large sections up to and including Bhamdoun, composed of four lanes, separated by a central barrier.

Price of petrol: 36.25 Lebanese piastres per litre for super.

ATCL, Fattal Building, rue du Port at Beirut.
Open from 8.30 a.m. to 12.30, and from 3 p.m. to 6 excepting Saturdays, open from 8.30 a.m. to 12.30.

Self-drive cars, without chauffeur. (i.e.: Hertz 1973)
Volkswagen 1300, LL 16 per day, plus LP 19 per km.
Fiat 125, r 16 Peugeot 504, LL 19 per day, plus LP 22 per km.
Volvo, Valiant, Dodge, LL 26 per day, plus LP 26 per km.

organized tours

A large number of tourist agencies throughout the country sell "organized tours" of Lebanon lasting from one week to a month; these tours include visits to the high spots of Lebanese tourist attractions such as Baalbek, Tyre, Saida, Jeita and Anjar... Some organizations organize regular commented tours with small groups of tourists conducted by extremely competent guides.

The ordinary organized tour, based on the assumption that the tourist only wants "the sun and the sea", includes a more or less lengthy stay at Beirut, from whence outings never exceeding one day (except for visits to Syria) are undertaken. This, for example is what one of the Beirut agencies offers: tour of Beirut (half-day, LL 7); Nahr al-Kalb and Byblos (half-day, LL 10); grotto of Jeita and Byblos (half-day, LL 17); the Cedars and Tripoli (half-day, LL 32); grotto of Jeita and the Jounie-Hassar teleferic (half-day, LL 20); Baalbek and Anjar (one day, LL 25); Beit ed-Dine, Saida and Sour (one day, LL 32); Saida and Sour (one day, LL 30); Beit ed-Dine and Saida (half-day, LL 18); Beirut by night (LL 32); the Lebanese Casino (LL 40 with two drinks, LL 62 with dinner).

THE PORT OF BEIRUT

3,594 ships of all categories, representing a tonnage of 5,998,005 tons, called at the port of Beirut during 1972. 2,666,721 tons of merchandise were unloaded and 667,378 tons loaded, making a total movement of 3,344,199 tons. "Beirut, ever since olden times, has always been considered to be the "Door of the Orient". But, apart from its geographical position, the privileged situation which its port continues to enjoy is due to three principal factors.

The first in importance of these factors is circumstantial: the closing of the Suez Canal which blocked the maritime route to the ports beyond the Red Sea. It is found to be advantageous to send shipments destined to these ports in transit to Beirut and from there by land, rather than to take the long sea journey by way of the Cape of Good Hope. This explains, in particular, why the greater part of Saudi Arabian imports, as also those of the Gulf Emirates and even those of Irak, transit today by the Lebanese port.

The other two factors are particular to Lebanon. They are due to the facilities offered to transit shipments. Firstly, the port facilities of equipment and formalities, which it would be useless to try to find elsewhere in that part of the Mediterrannean. Secondly, the political conjuncture which prevails in the country, and the economic relations which the Lebanese know so well how to arrange everywhere in the world (...) Lebanon will always remain a haven of peace and stability."

AJAX
"Le Commerce du Levant",
special issue

TRAVEL AGENCIES MEMBERS OF IATA

AMLEVCO - Rue de Phénicie Tel: 233830	MASSOUD TRAVEL - Rue Rian Solh Tel: 232777
AMERICAN EXPRESS, Amlevco Tours Tel: 220397	NAWAS TOURIST AGENCY, - Riad Solh Tel: 240285
A.K.S., Souk Tawilé, Tel: 225271	NAWAS TOURIST AGENCY, - rue Sadat Tel: 346060
BEIRUT EXPRESS CO - Rue d'Artois tel: 341400	NEAR EAST EXPRESS - Rue Hamra Tel: 341995
COMET - Rue Makdessi Tel: 340240	SAAD TRANSPORT - rue B. el Khoury Tel: 232312
THOMAS COOK & SON - Starco Building Tel: 220358	INTERTOUR TRAVCO - Rue de Verdun Tel: 353090
DEBBAS O.D. - Rue Kantari Tel: 240200	USI - United Services Internatio-nal Tel: 341150
EASTMAR - Avenue des Français Tel: 230619	LEBANON-EXPRESS - Avenue des Français Tel: 227025
GLOBE TOURS S.A.L. - Rue de Phénicie Tel: 295585	
KURBAN TOURS - Rue Riad Solh Tel: 240240	
KLAT TRAVEL, Starco Centre, Tel: 235663	
LEVON TRAVEL BUREAU, - rue Hamra Tel. 347140	
LEVON TRAVEL BUREAU, - Riad Solh Tel. 256942	

circuits

Lebanon in three days (1)

First day: Beirut, Saida, Tyre (lunch), Beit ed-Dine (overnight stay at Deir el-Qamar).

Second day: tour of Beit ed-Dine or Deir el-Qamar, Barouk (lunch and walk in the cedar forest), Aamiq (the road from Barouk to Aamiq is not shown on the maps), Qaraoun Lake (there and back), Chtaura, Anjar, Chtaura (overnight stay).

Third day: Chtaura, Baalbek, the Cedars via the Ainata pass, Becharre (lunch), Tripoli, Jbail (Byblos), Beirut.

Lebanon in three days (2)

First day: Beirut, Jbail (Byblos), Batroun, Tripoli (lunch and tour of town), the Cedars, Becharre (overnight stay).

Second day: Becharre, Baalbek, Zahle (lunch), Chtaura, Anjar, Beit ed-Dine, Deir el-Qamar (overnight stay).

Third day: Deir el-Qamar or Beit ed-Dine, Jezzine, Beaufort Castle, Tyre (lunch), Saida, Beirut.

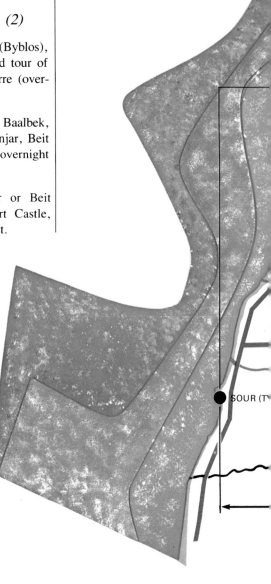

SOUR (T

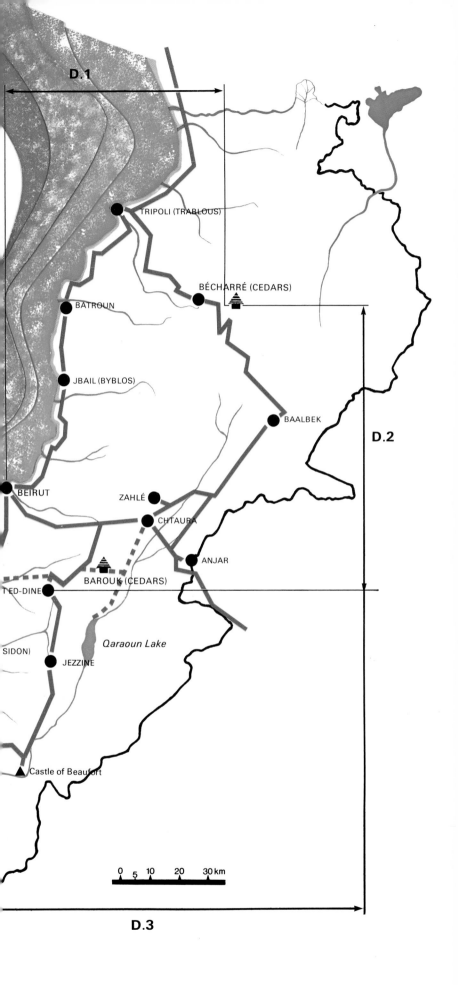

D.1

TRIPOLI (TRABLOUS)

BÉCHARRÉ (CEDARS)

BATROUN

JBAIL (BYBLOS)

BAALBEK

D.2

BEIRUT

ZAHLÉ

CHTAURA

ANJAR

BAROUK (CEDARS)

T ED-DINE

SIDON)

JEZZINE

Qaraoun Lake

▲ Castle of Beaufort

0 5 10   20   30 km

D.3

Lebanon in seven days (1)

First day: Beirut, Saida (tour and lunch), Tyre (tour and overnight stay); possibility of returning to Saida, Joun and the Deir al-Moukhalless convent (tomb of Lady Stanhope). Return to Beirut for the night.

Second day: Tyre, Nabatiye (large township typical of southern Lebanon), Beaufort Castle, Jezzine (lunch), Moukhtara and Deir el-Qamar, Beit ed-Dine (overnight stay).

Third day: Tour of Deir el-Qamar or Beit ed-Dine, Barouk (lunch after touring the Cedars), Aamiq, Chtaura or Zahle (overnight stay).

Fourth day: Anjar, Baalbek (lunch and overnight stay).

Fifth day: Baalbek, the Cedars, Becharre (lunch), Ehden, Tripoli (overnight stay).

Sixth day: Tour of the Akkar: Halba, Qoubbayat, Qammoua plateau (picnic), Fneidek, Tripoli (overnight stay).

Seventh day: Tripoli, Deir al-Balamend, Jbail (lunch), Jeita, Beirut.

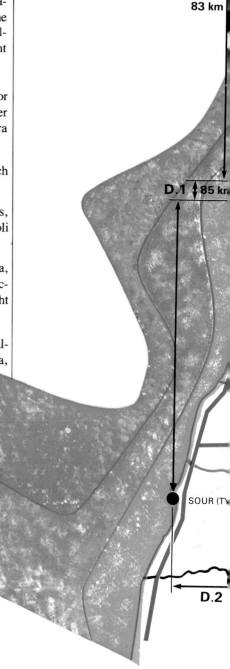

D.7
83 km

D.1 85 km

SOUR (T

D.2

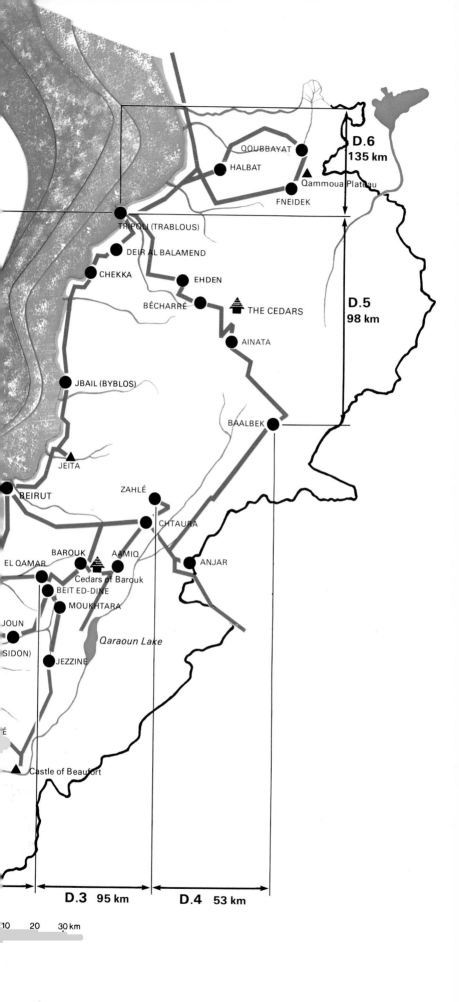

QOUBBAYAT

HALBAT

FNEIDEK

Qammoua Plateau

D.6
135 km

TRIPOLI (TRABLOUS)

DEIR AL BALAMEND

CHEKKA

EHDEN

BÉCHARRÉ

THE CEDARS

D.5
98 km

AINATA

JBAIL (BYBLOS)

BAALBEK

JEITA

BEIRUT

ZAHLÉ

CHTAURA

BAROUK   AAMIQ

EL QAMAR

ANJAR

Cedars of Barouk

BEIT ED-DINE

MOUKHTARA

JOUN

Qaraoun Lake

SIDON)

JEZZINE

É

Castle of Beaufort

D.3 95 km

D.4 53 km

10   20   30 km

Lebanon in seven days (2)

First day: Beirut, Jeita, Jbail (lunch), Afqa, Kartaba (overnight stay).

Second day: Kartaba, Laklouk, Batroun, Mseilha, Deir al-Balamend, Tripoli (lunch, tour and overnight stay).

Third day: Tour of the Akkar: Tripoli, Halba, Qoubbayat, Qammoua plateau (picnic), Fneidek, Tripoli (overnight stay).

Fourth day: Tripoli, Sir ed-Danniye, Sfire, Sir ed-Danniye (lunch), Zghorta, Ehden, Becharre, the Cedars, Becharre (overnight stay).

Fifth day: Becharre, Baalbek (lunch), Zahle, Chtaura, Anjar, Zahle (overnight stay).

Sixth day: Zahle, Qaraoun Lake, Jezzine (lunch), Beaufort Castle, Nabatiye, return to Jezzine for overnight stay until a hotel is built at Tyre.

Seventh day: Tyre, or Jezzine, Saida (lunch), Deir el-Qamar, Beit ed-Dine, Sofar, Aley, Beirut.

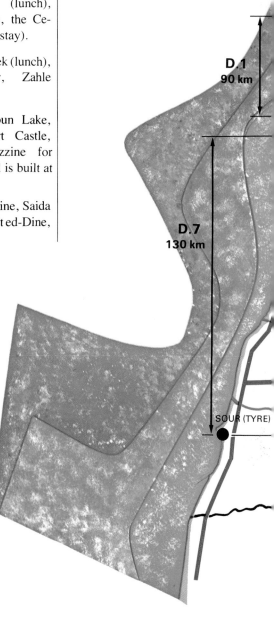

D
104

D.1
90 km

D.7
130 km

SOUR (TYRE)

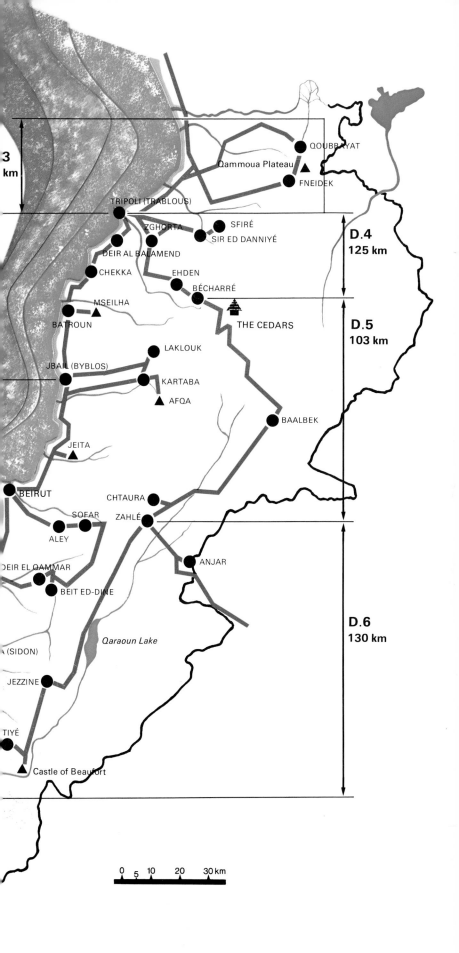

3 km

QOUBBAYAT

Qammoua Plateau

FNEIDEK

TRIPOLI (TRABLOUS)

ZGHORTA

SFIRÉ

SIR ED DANNIYÉ

DEIR AL BALAMEND

CHEKKA

EHDEN

BÉCHARRÉ

MSEILHA

THE CEDARS

BATROUN

LAKLOUK

JBAIL (BYBLOS)

KARTABA

AFQA

BAALBEK

JEITA

BEIRUT

CHTAURA

SOFAR

ZAHLÉ

ALEY

ANJAR

DEIR EL QAMMAR

BEIT ED-DINE

Qaraoun Lake

D.6
130 km

(SIDON)

JEZZINE

TIYÉ

Castle of Beaufort

D.4
125 km

D.5
103 km

0 5 10   20   30 km

Lebanon in fourteen days

First day: Beirut, Aley, Bhamdoun, Sofar (very popular summer holiday resorts), Ain Zhalta, Barouk (lunch), Deir el-Qamar (overnight stay).

Second day: Deir el-Qamar, Damour, Deir el-Qamar, Beit ed-Dine, Barouk (lunch and tour of cedar forest), Cedars of Maasser ech-Chouf, Moukhtara, Aamatour, Baadarane, Niha, Jezzine (overnight stay).

Third day: Jezzine, Deir al-Moukhalless (tomb of Lady Stanhope), Joun, Saida (lunch, tour and overnight stay).

Fourth day: Saida, Tyre (tour) and overnight stay at Jezzine until a hotel is built at Tyre.

Fifth day: Tyre or Jezzine, Nabatiye, Beaufort Castle, Jezzine (lunch), Machghara, Qaraoun Lake, Chtaura (overnight stay).

Sixth day: Chtaura, Anjar, Zahle (lunch), temples of Niha, Antoura, Dhour ech-Choueir (overnight stay).

Seventh day: Dhour ech-Choueir, Zahle, Baalbek (lunch, tour and overnight stay).

Eighth day: Baalbek, Fakehe (handmade carpets), Deir Mar Maroun (grotto of Saint Maron and sources of the Orontes), Pyramid of Hermel (Qanouat al-Hermel), Hermel (lunch), Steles of Nebuchadnezzar, return to Baalbek (overnight stay).

Ninth day: Baalbek, the Cedars, Becharre (lunch), grotto and valley of the Kadisha, Becharre (overnight stay).

Tenth day: Becharre, Hasroun, Hadet ej-Jobbe (forest of cedars and lunch), Kousba, Amioun, Chekka, Tripoli (overnight stay).

Eleventh day: Tripoli, Ehden, Becharre, Ehden (lunch), Zghorta, Sir ed-Danniye, Sfire, Tripoli (overnight stay).

Twelfth day: Tour of the Akkar: Halba, Qoubbayat, Qammoua plateau (picnic), Fneidek, Tripoli, Jbail (overnight stay).

Thirteenth day: Jbail, Laklouk (lunch), Afqa, Kartaba, Jbail (overnight stay).

Fourteenth day: Jbail, Jounie, Sarba, Harissa (Our Lady of Lebanon, view over the Bay of Jounie), Meyouba, Faraya (lunch), natural bridge over the Nahr al-Laban, Fakra, Nahr al-Kalb, Jeita, Beirut.

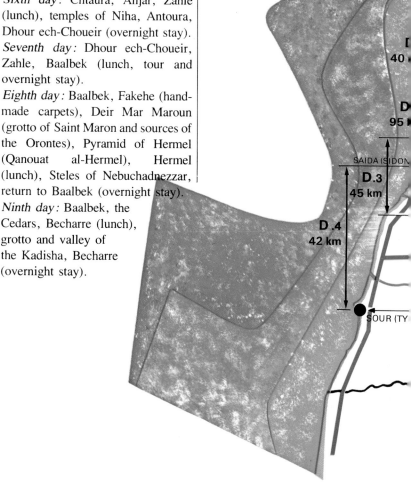

BE

D
40

D
95

SAIDA (SIDON

D.3
45 km

D.4
42 km

SOUR (TY

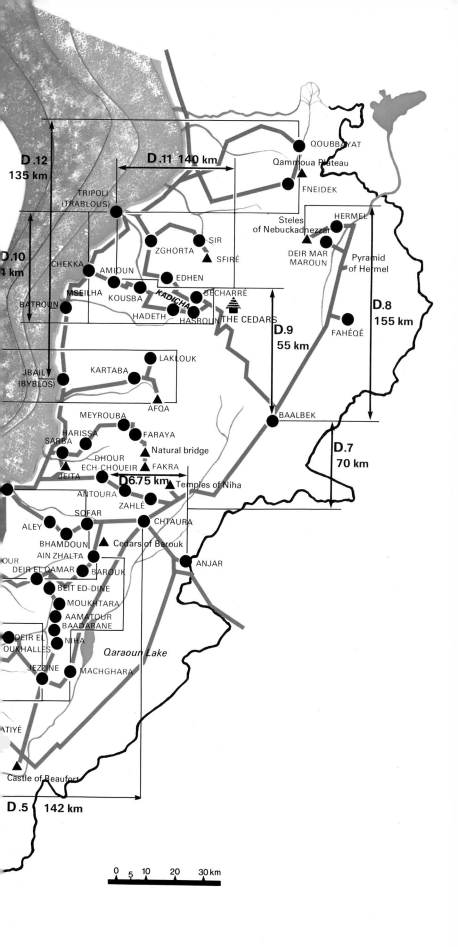

D .12
135 km

D .11 140 km

QOUBBAYAT
Qammoua Plateau
FNEIDEK

TRIPOLI
(TRABLOUS)

Steles
of Nebuckadnezzar

HERMEL

DEIR MAR
MAROUN

Pyramid
of Hermel

D.10
1 km

CHEKKA
AMIOUN
ZGHORTA
SIR
SFIRÉ
EDHEN
MSEILHA
KOUSBA
KADICHA
BÉCHARRÉ
BATROUN
HADETH
HASROUN THE CEDARS

D.9
55 km

D.8
155 km

FAHÉQÉ

LAKLOUK
JBAIL
(BYBLOS)
KARTABA
AFQA

D.7
70 km

MEYROUBA
BAALBEK
HARISSA
SARBA
FARAYA
Natural bridge
DHOUR
ECH-CHOUEIR FAKRA
JEITA
D6.75 km Temples of Niha
ANTOURA
ZAHLÉ
SOFAR
ALEY
CHTAURA
BHAMDOUN
Cedars of Barouk
AIN ZHALTA
OUR
DEIR EL QAMAR
BAROUK
ANJAR
BEIT ED-DINE
MOUKHTARA
AAMATOUR
BAADARANE
DEIR EL
OUKHALLES
NIHA
Qaraoun Lake
JEZZINE
MACHGHARA

ATIYÉ

Castle of Beaufort

D .5 142 km

0 5 10 20 30 km

excursions

Three excursions from Beirut

(1) Saida, Jezzine, Machghara (on the other side of the Lebanon by an ill-kept road), Qaraoun Lake, Aamiq, Chtaura, Beirut. A long day.

(2) Jeita, Faraya (natural bridge over the Nahr al-Laban and temples of Fakra), Rayfoun, Harissa (Our Lady of Lebanon, view over the Bay of Jounie), Jounie, Beirut. Can be done in a day or half a day.

(3) Beirut, Jbail (Byblos), Tripoli and back. One day.

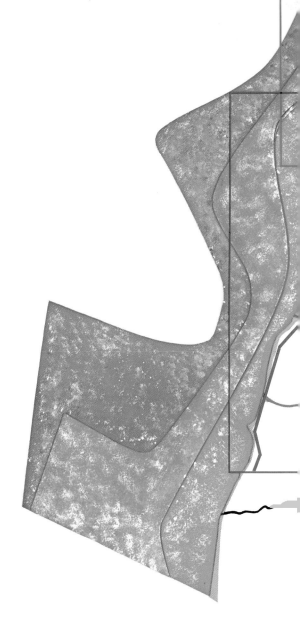

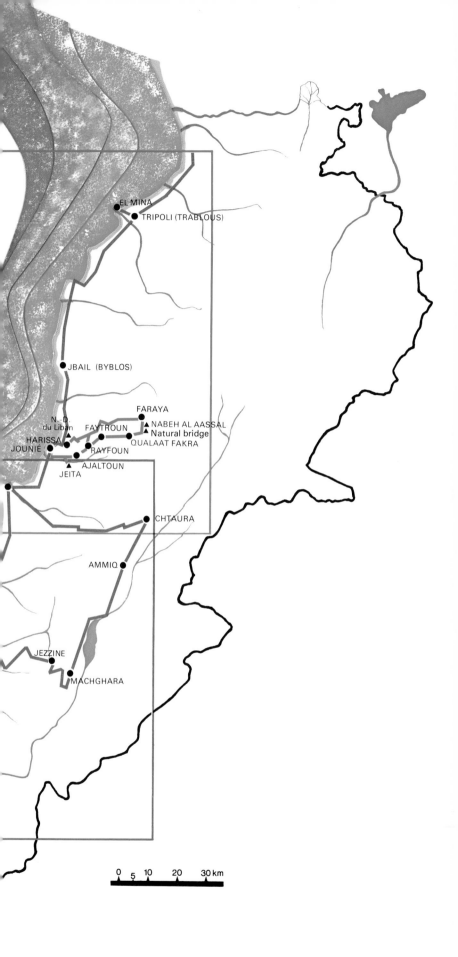

EL MINA
TRIPOLI (TRABLOUS)

JBAIL (BYBLOS)

FARAYA
N.-D. du Liban ▲ NABEH AL AASSAL
FAYTROUN ▲ Natural bridge
HARISSA QUALAAT FAKRA
JOUNIÉ RAYFOUN
▲ AJALTOUN
JEITA

CHTAURA

AMMIQ

JEZZINE
MACHGHARA

0 5 10   20   30 km

Excursions from Tripoli

(1) Halba (large market, centre of the Akkar plateau), Qoubbayat (fine Arab palace at Bire, 4 km before Qoubbayat), Qammoua plateau (springs, nomad camps, fine pine-trees, many pleasant walks, but the road from Qoubbayat to Qammoua is in a poor state of repair), Fneidek (village inhabited by somewhat wild mountain-dwellers), Tripoli. A good day.

(2) Zghorta, Ehden, Becharre, Hasroun, Hadeth ej-Jobbe (forest), Amioun (old houses), Deir al-Balamend, Tripoli. One day.

(3) Sir ed-Danniye, Sfire, sources of Nabeh Soukkar, fine cliffs of the Wadi Soukkar, and back. Half a day.

Excursions from Deir El-Qamar

(1) Damour, Saida and the temple of Echmoun, Tyre and back. One day.

(2) Beit ed-Dine, Moukhtara (palace of Jumblatt and back. Half a day.

(3) Barouk, Cedars of Barouk, Cedars of Maasser ech-Chouf, Baadarane (former palace of Ali Pasha Jumblatt), Aamatour (former house of Abu Shakra, source and waterfall of Ain Mourched), Niha (strategic grotto of Chekif Tiroun, an hour's walk to get to the grotto), return via Moukhtara. One day.

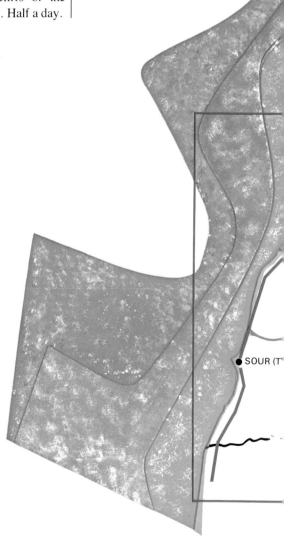

SOUR (T

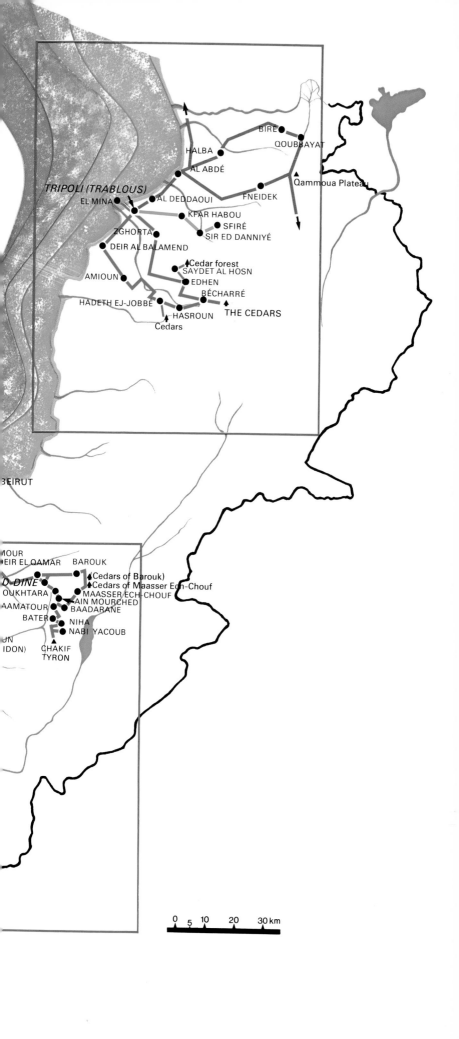

BIRE

QOUBBAYAT

HALBA

AL ABDÉ

Qammoua Plateau

TRIPOLI (TRABLOUS)

EL MINA

AL DEDDAOUI

FNEIDEK

KFAR HABOU

SFIRÉ

ZGHORTA

SIR ED DANNIYÉ

DEIR AL BALAMEND

▲Cedar forest
SAYDET AL HOSN

AMIOUN

EDHEN

BÉCHARRÉ

HADETH EJ-JOBBÉ

THE CEDARS▲

HASROUN
▲
Cedars

BEIRUT

MOUR
EIR EL QAMAR   BAROUK

D-DINE   ▲(Cedars of Barouk)
OUKHTARA   ▲Cedars of Maasser Ech-Chouf
                          MAASSER ECH-CHOUF
AAMATOUR   AIN MOURCHED
                        BAADARANE
      BATER   NIHA
                    NABI YACOUB
JN
IDON)   CHAKIF
          TYRON▲

0   5 10   20   30 km

Excursions from Becharre

(1) Hasroun (interesting village, fine cliffs of the Kadisha), Hadeth ej-Jobbe (go further on to the fine forest of cedars where you can take a long walk), Tannourine el-Faouqa (lovely village and fine forest), return to Becharre. One day.

(2) Valley of the Kadisha, Deir Qannoubine, famous Maronite monastery in the cliffs, the seat of the Patriarchate from the fifteenth to the nineteenth centuries to which pilgrimages are made (walk in the bottom of the valley). Half a day or a whole day, depending on the length of the walk.

(3) Cedars, teleferic, ascent of Kornet es-Saouda (three hours, walk), and back. One day.

(4) Ehden, Saydet al-Hosn (whence you arrive at the fine forest with its variety of trees and sources). Half a day or a day.

Excursions from Laklouk or Kartaba

(1) Grand Hotel, Laklouk, Tannourine el-Faouqa road. At a distance of 1 km, houses cut in the cliffs (La Bergerie), at 5 km, two chasms, Tannourine el-Faouqa (pretty houses), Douma (large emigrant village with fine Lebanese houses), Jaj (after 3 km of bad road, the beautiful cedars of Jaj), Mechmech, Annaya (tomb of Father Charbel, pilgrimage), Ehmej (beautiful village), back to Laklouk (and Kartaba) by a road through a canyon. One day.

(2) Laklouk (or Kartaba), Afqa, Aqoura (grottoes of Roueiss, of interest to pot-holers), Roman road to Lake Yammoune on the eastern slope of the Lebanon), Laklouk via Arab el-Laklouk (new road), Kartaba. Half a day.

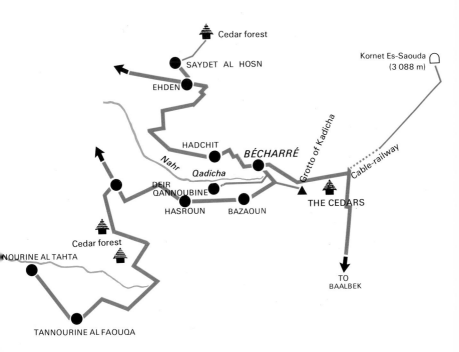

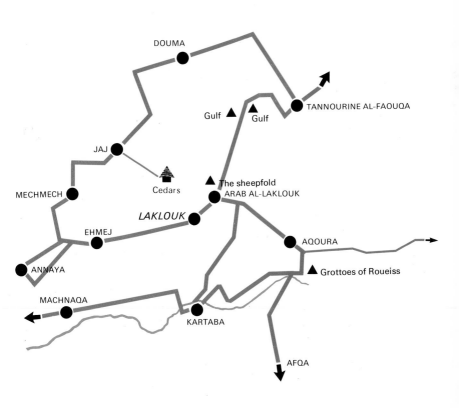

Excursions from Chtaura

(1) Anjar, Rayak, Niha (temples), Zahle, Chtaura. Half a day or a whole day with lunch at Zahle and a tour of the town.

(2) Baalbek, Fakehe (hand-made carpets), Deir Mar Maroun (grottoes of Saint Maron, sources of the Orontes), pyramid of Hermel, Hermel and back. If possible, go as far as the Steles of Nebuchadnezzar. A long day.

(3) Aamiq (pretty wood), Lake Qaraoun, Sehmor and Yohmor (walk through the gorges of the Litani, two hours there and back), Ebles Saki, Souk el-Kahn (Druze market every Tuesday morning), Hasbaya (Chehab palace, weaving of Druze coats), Rachaya (fortress where Bichara al Khury and Riad el Solh were imprisoned), Es Souaire. A long day.

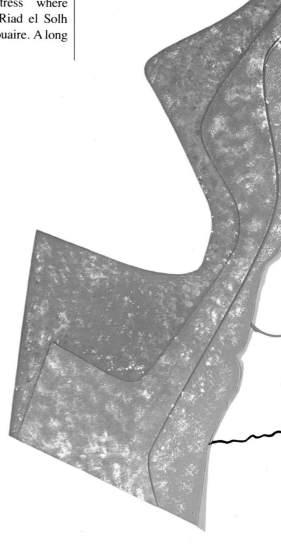

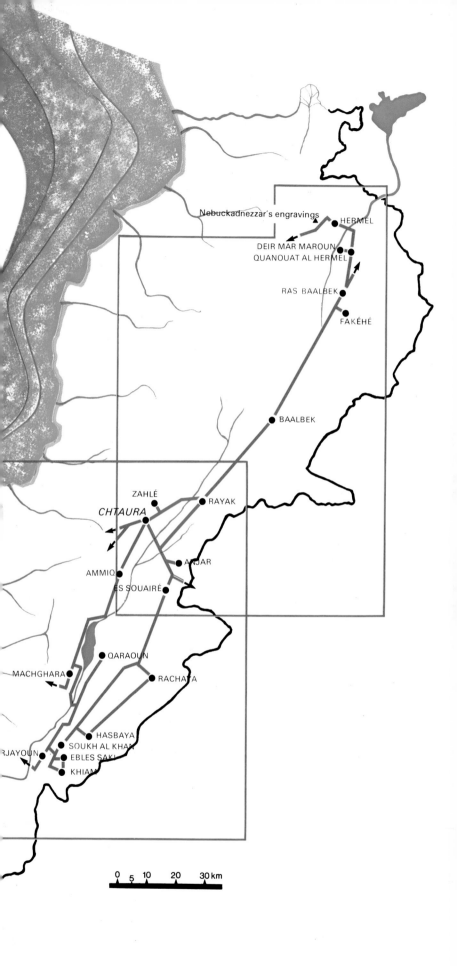

Nebuckadnezzar's engravings

HERMEL

DEIR MAR MAROUN
QUANOUAT AL HERMEL

RAS BAALBEK

FAKÉHÉ

BAALBEK

ZAHLÉ   RAYAK

CHTAURA

ANJAR

AMMIQ
ES SOUAIRÉ

QARAOUN

MACHGHARA   RACHAYA

HASBAYA
SOUKH AL KHAN
EBLES SAKI
RJAYOUN
KHIAM

0 5 10   20   30 km

lebanon for young people

The National Tourist Council set up in 1963 a Tourist Board for Young People, where there is a most remarkable atmosphere and flurry of activity... The Board has premises where young people of all nationalities are received, advised and guided towards original forms of tourism or occupation.

In this way young people are diverted from the stereotyped and irksome forms of tourism and, if they wish, placed in direct contact with the population of the country by means of invitations to visit families, meetings with young Lebanese, and participation in discussions, the Baalbek International Festival and international work sites and workshops. They can attend popular events organized by the Tourist Board and recitals of Oriental music, as well as taking part in tours.

Students, and other young people interested, can study Arabic at a specialized centre and participate in workshops on the various aspects of Arab civilization and in archaeological seminars.

The Board runs a dozen hostels (which are extremely cheap — LL 2 to 3 per night) in various parts of Lebanon, and sends young people with very little money to spare to youth hostels (LL 2), very cheap hotels (LL6), camping sites (LL1.5) and restaurants serving meals at LL 2 or 3, etc.

One of the most original organizations, and most appreciated by young people who have tried it, is that of the Lebanese Craft Holidays, which was the result of an idea of Constantin Malliarudakis and is sponsored by the Youth Tourist Board.

CAMPING IN LEBANON

Camping is free. It is even possible to camp on private ground, provided that permission is requested beforehand from the proprietor. It is preferable, however, to keep to the camping grounds approved by the CNT, of which a list is given hereunder:

■ Beirut — Armand de Chayla University Camping Centre, Rue de Damas, near to the National Museum. Open throughout the year. LL 2 per night, car LL 5 whatever the length of the stay. University restaurant facilities available (menu LL 2.50)

■ Aamchit — (Byblos) "Les Colombes", at 38 km north of Beirut. Proprietor, Malek Fares Lahud — Tel: Jbail 940322. LL 1.25 per night per person, parking LL 0.50. Rent of tent for two, LL 2 per night. — On leaving Byblos, in the direction of Tripoli, at a distance of 500 m. after the bridge, the camping site is situated between the sea and the national road where this forks for Aamchit.

■ Byblos — "Mocamp", Société des Centres Touristiques du Liban — 35 km north of Beirut, near the old part of Byblos. LL 1 per night per person in the camping, Ll 3 per person in rooms with 2 or 3 beds. Free parking, free hot water and use of kitchen stove.

Previous page:
The Lebanese coast offers all the pleasures of the sea.
(Photo: MEA.)

In Mar Challita, a wonderful old disused monastery, which young people have rendered habitable, situated in one of the most beautiful landscapes of this grandiosely arid region, not far from Jounie, young people from all countries come on very free-and-easy-training courses, living in a sort of joyous phalanstery inspired by the warmth of character of Contantin Malliarudakis. The course lasts from 5 to 12 days (and can be prolonged if space is available), during which trainees are initiated into the various crafts (wickerwork, weaving, carpentry, wood carving, silk printing, pottery, enamel, etc.). The price for a twelve day course varies from 35 to 45 dollars according to circumstances.

The adresses of the organisations quoted are as follows:
Youth Tourist Board: Ghanem Building, Rue de Verdun, above the Bustros Pharmacy. B.P. 5344, Beirut. Cables: TOULIBAN. Tel.: 220 285.
Offices open from 8 a.m. to 8 p.m. in July and August and from 8 a.m. to 2 p.m. the rest of the year.
Lebanese Craft Holidays: Constantin Malliarudakis, B.P. 89, Jounie.

■ Sarafand — (Saida) "Sarepta", 55 km south of Beirut. LL 1 per night. Proprietor: Haidar Khalife — On leaving Saida, in the direction of Tyre, at a distance of 10 km, the camping ground is situated on the beach at the level of the first café after the Shell petrol-station.

■ Sour (Tyre) — Rest House, Per night and bathing LL 2, Rooms with two beds, very comfortable, LL 10 per person. Tel: 740677. The camping site is situated close to the excavations ground. Cars and caravans must park in the parking site.

■ Khaïzaran — "Kasr el Bahr", 65 km south of Beirut, in the direction of Sour. Proprietors, Hassan et Hussein Fakih, Tel: Sarafand N° 2. LL 1 per night. Bungalow (3-4 beds) LL 2 per person.

■ Baalbek — "La Source". Proprietor, Khawam, Hotel de la Source. Tel: Baalbek 22. Ask for La Source Ras el Aïn. LL 1 per night.

■ Deir Zeinoun — (near to the Syrian frontier on the road to Damascus) "Vert Bocage", 55 km from Beirut. Proprietor, Michel Elias Kahde. Tel: 841001 - 841023. LL1 per night.

All of these camping-grounds are open throughout the year. There accommodation for caravans, but none of them is equipped for the supply of water, electricity or drainage. For all information, apply to BTJ, Rue de Rome, Quartier Sanayeh, Tel: 220285.
If in difficulties on the road or in the camp, contact the Tourist Police, tel: 343286.

your stay in lebanon

How to get information

The Lebanese National Tourist Council is the most authorized source of information in the country. In Lebanon itself, the visitor will have little difficulty in making himself understood, except in remote mountainous areas (and even here good will and good manners will enable him to overcome the language difficulty), for he will find everywhere people who speak and understand French or English.

Beirut presents no problem. Most shop-signs are in Arabic and French or Arabic and English... Bills are made out in French and English. The Lebanese has a reputation for being a polyglot and likes to help.

When to come to Lebanon

The best answer is: "all the year round". In summer, Lebanon provides all the pleasures of the sea and beaches as well as those of the mountain (international holiday centres with casinos, entertainments of all sorts, excursions, festivals and so on).

In winter, this mountainous country provides its winter-sports centres. In the spring, the sporting tourist can ski in the morning and bathe in the sea in the afternoon. Autumn is ideal for outings, but anyone who wants to enjoy the beauty of deeply moving landscapes must come in the spring or autumn, on account of the purity of the atmosphere and the excellent visibility (in summer, the mountain is nearly always shrouded in mist). In spring, too, there is the wonderful, extraordinary flowering of an extremely varied vegetation, with its accompaniment of perfumes. It is hot in Lebanon in summer, and there is no rain from June to September. But

THE NATIONAL TOURIST COUNCIL

The Lebanese Tourist Council (CNT) is a very active organization which makes very efficient efforts to promote an original tourist policy going beyond the traditional, stereotyped framework. It is able to provide inestimable help to those visitors who are interested in Lebanon as a whole, its present and past history, its human and archaeological riches. It has established offices in nine different countries, where tourists can obtain excellent information and documentation before beginning their journey. It also publishes a monthly journal, "Liban Gazette", notifying the cultural events taking place during the month, and containing articles of information for tourists. The address of the CNT, and also those of its offices in foreign countries, are given below:

■ Conseil National du Tourisme
Rue de la Banque du Liban
Beirut, Lebanon. B.P. 5344,
Tel: 343175.

■ Office du Tourisme Libanais
18 Rue Ravenstein
Brussels, Belgium.
Tel: 134923, Telex: 26266
Cable: Ambaliban Brussels.

■ Lebanon Tourist and Information Office
1 Talaat Harb Street (Midan al-Tahrir)
Cairo, Arab Republic of Egypt
Tel: 30479
Cable: Legaban.

■ Offizielles Libanesisches Fremdenverkehrsbüro
46 Baselerstrasse
Francfurt, Federal German Republic.
Tel: 234644 & 235987, Telex 416339
Cable: Touliban Frankfurt.

nights in the mountain are often cold. Those attending the Baalbek festival should bring plenty of woollies.

Frontier formalities

A visa is required for all travellers entering Lebanon except those from Arab countries. Visas are valid three months for two journeys or six months for several journeys. They are issued by Lebanese consulates and on arrival at the airport. An exit visa is required after a stay of more than three months. It should be noted that the Lebanese Government refuses admission to holders of Israeli passports and, strictly speaking, to holders of any passport containing a visa for Israel, whether valid or expired and whether used or not.

All travellers are required to present a certificate of vaccination against smallpox, while those from regions where yellow fever or cholera are endemic are required to present certificates of vaccination against these diseases.

The Lebanese customs allow the duty-free import of 500 cigarettes and 500 grams of tobacco from 1 June to 31 October, and 200 cigarettes and 200 grams of tobacco from 1 November to 31 May, one litre of alcoholic drink and a "reasonable" quantity of perfume. The import of narcotics is strictly forbidden, and a licence is required for the export of antiquities. Any amount of money in any currency may be either imported or exported.

■ Lebanon Tourist and Information Office
c/o Lebanese Embassy
Medina Avenue
Jeddah, Saudi Arabia.
B.P. 987, Tel: 52696

■ Lebanon Tourist and Information Office
c/o Lebanese Embassy
Istiklal Street
Kuwait.
B.P. 253, Tel: 613818

■ Lebanon Tourist and Information Office
c/o Lebanese Embassy
21 Kensington Palace Gardens
London, United Kingdom.
Tel: 7265/6, Telex 262048

■ Lebanon Tourist and Information Office
405, Park Avenue
New York, N.Y. 10022, U.S.A.
Tel: (212) 421 - 2201 - 2
Cable: Touliban, New York.

■ Bureau de Tourisme Libanais
124 Faubourg Saint-Honoré
75008 Paris France
Tel: 3591036, Telex 66016F
Cable: Touliban Paris 008.

■ Libanesika Turisbyran
Engelbrektsplan 2
S-11432, Stockholm, Sweden.
Tel: 119650 & 119651, Telex: 17555
Cable: Touliban Stockholm.

hotels around beirut

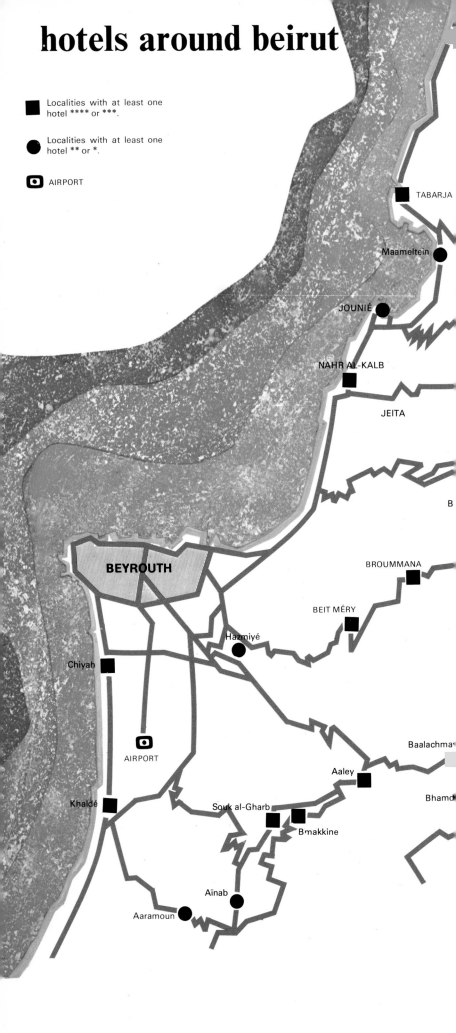

■ Localities with at least one hotel **** or ***.

● Localities with at least one hotel ** or *.

▣ AIRPORT

TABARJA

Maameltein

JOUNIÉ

NAHR AL-KALB

JEITA

B

BEYROUTH

BROUMMANA

BEIT MÉRY

Hazmiyé

Chiyah

AIRPORT

Baalachma

Aaley

Khaldé

Bhamd

Souk al-Gharb

Bmakkine

Aïnab

Aaramoun

Jouret et Termoss

Kfour

Aachqout Faïtroun

Rayfoun

B

Bikfaya

Khinchara

Dhour ech Choueir Bolognia
(Bois de Boulogne)

Falougha

Hammana

gare

Sofar

Accommodation

Lebanon has a remarkable and impressive hotel system, where Beirut and the international holiday centres are concerned. There are hotels of all categories, particularly first-class hotels which compare favourably with the best in Europe. In Beirut, the *Saint Georges*, the *Phoenicia* (Intercontinental) and the *Vendôme,* classified ****A by the Ministry of Tourism, are in fact international palaces.

The same applies to the *Park Hotel* at Chtaura and, above all, the Hotel *Al-Bustan* at Beit Mery. The latter, from the terrace of which there is a wonderful view of Beirut and the Mediterranean, and the 151 bedrooms and suites of which are all furnished in different styles, was meant to be an International Conference Centre. It has an auditorium capable of seating 460 with simultaneous interpretation equipment in four languages and two conference-rooms each with a capacity of 250.

Very fine hotel complexes have also been built on the beaches (Tabarja and Khalde) and at the winter-sports centres of Laklouk and Faraya.

Yet in spite of everything, too much effort has been devoted to Beirut. Tripoli has not a single hotel worthy of a city of 150,000 inhabitants. Nor has Saida. The tourist who wants to stop in one of the marvellous little towns dotted about the mountains, and wrongly ignored by the tourist circuits, usually finds only country inns which, though generally clean, lack comfort and warmth. On the other hand, he will find himself plunged into the most authentic Lebanese reality.

The communes listed below have hotels contained in the list of the chief hotels in Lebanon, page 216. (The localities described in "town by town" are in blocks capitals).

eating

The Lebanese love eating, and their cooking is rich and often complicated. However, the impersonal, international food of the big hotels and the ''snack'' type of eating, which exists in all countries, are gaining ground. The Lebanese cooking suffers from the severe handicap of not having good beef at its disposal. Only mutton is good and acceptable. Hence the trouble given to preparation and the vigourous seasoning. But what a variety of dishes!

Lebanese dishes

The *mezze* is a speciality which makes the visitor either enthusiastic or stupefied. Basically, the mezze is a selection of hors d'œuvre. But a good mezze consists of 30 to 40 dishes (some even claim as many as 80) and constitutes a very substantial meal in itself. Some of these dishes should always be present — *tabboule* (a salad of parsley, shallots, sliced tomatoes and crushed corn) which you eat with a lettuce leaf; *baba ghannouj* or *mtabal* (mashed grilled aubergines and sesame seeds) served with a dressing of olive oil; *hommos* (mashed chick-peas with sesame oil); *kebbe*, the most famous of all Lebanese dishes (finely chopped lamb and veal seasoned with crushed corn and served raw, fried or grilled); *labne* (a sort of white cheese made from yogurt); *fatayers* (triangular meat or spinach and pine-seeds fritters); and *waraq anab mehchi* (stuffed vine leaves). A mezze also includes lamb's brains, liver, marrow, goat cheese, olives, and many other strange things, guessing the origin of which is quite a game. Since the meat is of poor quality, all stuffings are welcome, including *koussa mehchi* (marrows stuffed with minced meat and rice cooked in a spicy tomato sauce). *Kafta* is minced and spiced meat eaten from a skewer, *chawarma* consists of slices of soused mutton grilled on a vertical skewer (very fat), *moughrabiye* is the Lebanese couscous, and *farrouj mechoui* is grilled chicken served with a garlic sauce. *Mechoui* is the best thing to ask for when you know nothing about a restaurant. Chicken on skewers and grilled chicks are also good.

By the seashore you can get excellent grilled fish, fish with piquant sauce, and *sayadiyeh*, a tasty dish consisting of pieces of fish cooked with onions, almonds, pine-seeds and spices served with brown rice. The most suitable bread is *khobz arabi* (Arab bread) or *marqouq* (very thin mountain bread as much as 40 cm in diameter, which can be folded like a napkin).

Desserts are rich and very sugary. Particular mention should be made of *ousmalliye* malliye (strings of crisp semolina dipped in cream or white cheese), and *ma'mouls*, the traditional Easter dish (small fritters of semolina covered with pistachio-nuts, crushed nuts or dates and perfumed with orange-flower-water). Lebanon can provide the entire range of Mediterranean and sub-tropical fruits, which are excellent.

Drinks

Mezze should be eaten with *arak*, the anisated drink. For the rest of the meal there are the local beers (which are excellent) and imported ones, or Lebanese wines, such as *Ksara* and *Musar*.

As Scandinavian gastronomy offers its 'smoerbroads', the lebanese offers the 'mezzé', a choice of some thirty to forty various delicious entrées. (Photo NCT - Yetenegian.)

souvenirs of lebanon

Lebanon sells much more than it produces. This is true not only of the general economy but also of the souvenirs offered for sale to tourists, in addition to authentic Lebanese products, articles from Syria and India. This situation is explained more by purely commercial considerations and the will-deserved reputation of products from Damascus than by any short-comings on the part of Lebanese craftsmen. Their crafts have a great and fine tradition.

However, the copper workers of Tripoli (and the small village of Kalamoun near that city) continue to engrave beautiful trays, ewers, bowls and vases. Some of these very simple copper vessels, without any ornamentation, are of great beauty. Lebanese craftsmen also make fabrics and embroideries of excellent quality.

However, the articles which predominate in the souvenir shops are the caftans richly embroidered with heavy gold stripes and the finely woven abayas — oriental costumes of a striking richness and very difficult to wear. The visitor who wishes to buy less gaudy but equally typical souvenirs can select scarves, table-cloths and doilies. In this range of articles, however, the curiosity shops usually try to sell Damascus ware. The leather and skin crafts provide cushions, poufs, blotting-pads and hand-bags. There still exist in Lebanon three glass-blowing work-shops. Visitors will find beautiful coloured glassware but also articles of the opaline type. A wide range of pottery is made in accordance with ancient techniques. The finest products of this trade are probably the most humble, very simple utensils

with unpretentious shapes. Lebanese pottery is not at all expensive.

Those who are interested can purchase those amazing fossilized fishes, the ichthyoliths, which were discovered in the region of Jbail. They are sold at Jbail itself and in village grocery shops such as those in Elmej.

There remain antiques. In a country where the soil hides so many ancient remains, there are many of these (above all Hellenistic and Roman terra cottas). But there are also a lot of fakes, and authenticity is difficult to determine. Moreover, the visitor should remember that the export of antiques is subject to regulations and that no ancient object can be taken out of the country without the authorization of the General Department of Antiquities.

Buying souvenirs is always a difficult problem. It is rare for the enthusiastic purchaser not to be disappointed when a friend shows him the same article he has bought for half the price. To what extent should one bargain? That is the problem. If the tourist goes to the "Maison de l'Artisan" (Craftsmen House) in Beirut, a fine modern building at Minet el-Hosn where products of Lebanese craftsmen are exhibited and sold under State control, he will not have any disagreeable surprises. However, it is possible, by going direct to the craftsman or doing a little good-humoured bargaining with a shop-keeper, to get the same things cheaper.

Lebanon, like all other countries, offers both the best and the
worst of souvenirs to tourists. It is up to them to choose.
The market place of Deir el-Qamar.
(Photo M. Guillard.)

A very large number of Lebanese speak French or English fluently. Any tourist who finds that they don't have his accent or picks on a few faults of syntax and makes fun of them is just a stupid idiot. He is beyond hope and it is no good giving him any advice. Others will appreciate the ease with which so many Lebanese can express themselves in a foreign language. But let them not be tempted to give proof of an imaginary superiority by showing off their knowledge of events in the field of art and literature in the rest of the world. They will find plenty of Lebanese perfectly aware of these things.

In the first part of this book, I dealt at some length with the multiplicity of religions. The visitor, even if his views are sought, will do well not to enter into domestic disputes which, incidentally, are becoming increasingly rare.

The average Lebanese likes to know whom he is dealing with. He may therefore appear somewhat too inquisitive for the taste of some people. Do not get offended about questions which may appear to be indiscreet, for what may appear to be a lack of discretion is often merely a real interest and a desire to lay the foundations of true sympathy. Try, therefore, to avoid the issue by a courteous joke or a vague reply.

In the East, tipping (or baksheesh) is a custom of which everybody has at least heard. In this connection, Lebanon is different from other Middle East countries. There, backsheesh is reduced to the exact level of the tip in Latin countries. And even then only in the towns — which is to say Beirut. In the mountain people render service because they like doing so, without thought of reward. If a mountain-dweller refuses money you offer him in return for something he has done for you (and which you consider merits payment), do not

manners

*Lebanon produces the whole range of mediterranean and
subtropical fruit.*
(Photo NCT.)

insist; you will offend him.

It is perfectly ridiculous for an Englishman to eat nothing but ham and eggs or a Frenchman to eat nothing but steak and chips in Lebanon. The visitor will please his hosts by trying, without any display of anxiety, the various local dishes, many of which he will find delicious, and by mopping up the mashed aubergines, chick-peas or *labne* which are the essential accompaniment to any meal with his Arab bread (and not with his fork) when eating Lebanese *mezzes*.

The Lebanese is very clean and careful about his appearance. He does not appreciate either dirtiness or raggedness. The visitor of the hippy type would do well to remember this. Lastly, the visitor should be careful about his relations with the Lebanese, though these are nearly always excellent. The Lebanese are often particularly sensitive in their self-respect and their sense of what is right and proper; their susceptibility is often masked by their good breeding, but it may give rise to difficult situations.

THE "ZAIMS"

The ancestral families, who took refuge at one time in the citadel of the mountain, still have their followers. Humble peasants, small proprietors, even tradespeople, all depend more or less upon the "Zaïm" and always receive a welcome in the imposing house, with its lofty archways, whose appartments are wide open to the crowd.

What is a Zaïm exactly? This is what Andrée Chédid wrote in her excellent work on Lebanon: "The Zaïm, in the Lebanese sense of the term, is a political chief who has the support of a locally defined community which he exploits and, at the same time, protects. He generally belongs to a well-known family which has enjoyed considerable influence in the past... To be a Zaïm is not always a sinecure. Those who support him consider that they have certain rights where he is concerned; he is their creature... During the electoral period, the Zaïm's house is besieged as soon as day breaks by his electors. It is a hive..."

The legendary Lebanese hospitality beats all its records: one installs oneself and one welcomes the new arrivals as if one were in one's own house; one answers the telephone, one serves coffee, cool drinks, and copious meals are passed around. The Zaïm is on his divan, eyes half-closed, in front of a hookah, and listens to the commentaries, lays down political plans and, overflowing with affection, shakes hands unhurriedly with all. Each one present has the conviction that he is the Zaïm's dearest friend. The Zaïm's own success depends upon the personal attention and the time he consecrates to each one of his visitors.

PAUL CORON
"Liban, souriante splendeur"

daily life

Currency

The unit of currency is the Lebanese pound (LL). It is divided into 100 Lebanese piastres (LP). There are notes worth 100, 50, 25, 10, 5 and 1 pound (marked in Arabic on one side and Roman numerals on the other) and coins worth 50, 25, 10 and 5 piastres also marked in Arabic and Roman numerals.

In this country, where there is absolute freedom of exchange, where banks are many and money-changers legion, it is really very easy to change money. All hotels accept all currencies or will get them changed. The fairest rate of exchange is given by the banks. When dealing with the money-changers whose tiny counters decorated with notes in all currencies are everywhere to be seen in the commercial quarter, particularly around the Borj, you have to bargain.

Time

Local time is two hours ahead of Greenwich Mean Time, but Lebanon sometimes adopts summer time (one hour forward), as it did from June to September 1973.

Working hours in Lebanon are comparatively short (particularly during the month of Ramadan). The banks are open to the public from 8.30 a.m. to 12.30 from Monday to Friday and from 8.30 a.m. to midday on Saturday; exchange-offices from 9 a.m. to 12.30 and 3.30 p.m. to 6; and post-offices from 7 a.m. to 7 p.m. Public offices are open from 8 a.m. to 1.30 p.m. (Saturdays 8 a.m. to 12.30) in summer and 8 a.m. to 2 p.m. (Saturdays 8 a.m. to 1 p.m.) in winter; private offices from 8 a.m. to 1 p.m. and 3.30 p.m. to 6 in winter and 8 a.m. to 2 p.m. in summer.

Shops are usually open from 9 a.m. to 1.30 p.m. and 3.30 p.m. to 6, and bars from 8 p.m. to 4 a.m..

Prices

Taking into account a margin of uncertainty and the numerous exceptions involved, it may be estimated that prices in Lebanon, while not attaining those in Western Europe, are comparatively high. However, hotels are less expensive. In Beirut you pay from LL 40 to 80 for a room in a first class hotel, from LL 20 to 30 in an average one, and from LL 10 to 12 in a small but decent provincial one.

Western-type meals in fashionable restaurants are fairly expensive, but excellent Lebanese meals with excellent service can be had in good local restaurants. In Beirut itself, for example, at *Bahri's* near the harbour, where the food is very good, you get a meal for from LL 10 to 15. Service is included in hotel and restaurant bills, but it is usual to leave a little extra. Shops of a certain standing have fixed prices; elsewhere, haggling is the order of the day (particularly of course in the souks). As for the hawker who tries to sell you a scarf or a trinket, he himself would be disappointed if you didn't bargain with him.

Public services

Weights and measures: metric system. *Electricity:* 110 volts, with a few exceptions, particularly in the mountains.

The telephone service is good, but there are not many public telephones. You telephone from hotels, restaurants, cafés and service stations. The telephone is almost entirely automatic throughout the country. Local calls in Beirut cost 25 LP.

sport and amusements

Both sea and mountain get 300 days of sun a year. Lebanon where, in a quarter of an hour, you can go from the seashore to an altitude of 1,800 metres, is the ideal country for aquatic sports and skiing.

Aquatic sports

In Beirut, on the seashore and in the mountain all the big hotels have their own swimming-pool. There are some big aquatic sports centres; the biggest and the most exclusive is that of the *Lebanese Automobile and Touring Club* at Kaslik in the bay of Jounie (foreign visitors are admitted on production of their passports); there are also the *Saint-Georges Yacht and Motor Club*, just outside the Hotel Saint-Georges at Beirut, and the *Beirut Yachting Club* at the harbour. These clubs enable members to enjoy water-skiing, surfing and under-water fishing. For those who like bathing in fashionable surroundings there is a number of very fine private beaches at the south of Ramlet el-Beida in the suburbs of Beirut. In addition, there are large private communal beaches such as *Tabarja*. But the pretty little creeks, where not many people go, are very numerous, particularly on the northern coast.

Winter sports

Four centres are very well equipped: *the Cedars*, at 1,950 metres, where the snow is suitable for skiing from December to the end of April; *Faraya*, at 1,890 metres (December to end of April); *Kanat Bekiche*, at 1,990 metres, on the slopes of the Sannine (December to end of April); and *Laklouk*, at 1,750 metres (December to mid-April).

Other sports

There are two *golf clubs* — the Lebanon Golf Club at Beirut, and

Delmahiye south of the capital. *Horse-riding*, in this country of magnificent landscapes, is not sufficiently developed, though there are a few riding clubs. Nor is *tennis* played as much as might be expected in such a climate; there are about a dozen clubs, which issue temporary admission cards to foreign visitors.

Basket-ball is going out of fashion, but *football* is becoming very popular. The latter is played in municipal stadia, where the public gives vent to its feelings.

Quite recently, *motor rallies* have been introduced; they have been very popular, as was the case with the Lebanon-Syria rally (3,000 kms) in October 1972.

Amusements

Lebanon organizes a number of festivals. The foremost is that of Baalbek (July-August), which is of international repute. The Byblos festival is specialized in shows. The Beirut Film Festival alternates with that of Dinard. In 1973 a play festival was organized at Deir al-Qamar at the end of August by the Cultural and Technical Cooperation Agency, and a film festival was held at Beit Mery in September.

For those who like night life, Beirut has numerous night-clubs and popular art performances. Lebanon is also proud of having one of the largest casinos in the world. The Lebanese Casino, at Maamelteine 30 km north of Beirut, is as large and luxurious as the best to be found at Las Vegas. The revues in the vast "Ambassadors' Hall", performed before 850 diners, are worthy of a Cecil B. de Mille film. Those who prefer local colour can go to the working-class cabarets near the Place des Martyrs.

One could not speak of Beyrouth without mentioning its
night life.
(Photo NCT)

THE INTERNATIONAL FESTIVAL OF BAALBEK

Created in 1955, the International Festival of Baalbek has become one of the greatest cultural manifestations in the world. Although originally based on the French theatre, the Baalbek Festival has continued to increase the range of its spectacles, not only from the point of view of the type of shows offered, but also of the quality of the artists invited.

It now includes the French Theatre, the English Theatre, ballets, symphonic music, chamber music, jazz, spectacles of Lebanese folklore... theatre and ballet companies, and ensembles and soloists are chosen from amongst the most distinguished in the world.

During 1973, the following productions were presented: jazzman ·Miles Davis, the "Alvin Ailey City Center Dance Theater" from the USA, "The Prospect Theatre Company" from Great Britain, the pianist Claudio Arrau, the Chamber Music Orchestra of Jean-François Paillard, a Lebanese Folkloric Ensemble, the Mexican Folkloric Ballet, The State Symphonic Orchestra from the USSR.

This extremely fashionable and brilliant manifestation lasts for several weeks and takes place in three different scenes: the inside of the Temple of Bacchus for the Chamber Music, in front of the Temple of Bacchus for the ballets and the theatre, and the great courtyard of the Temple of Jupiter for the folkloric Spectacles.

*The temple of Bacchus provides a wonderful setting for the ballets
and concerts of the Baalbek International Festival.
(Photo NCT.)*

the lebanon hotels

LOCATION - altitude - distance from Beirut ESTABLISHMENTS	Category	Nb rooms	Tel.
AACHQOUT, 1050 m, 31 km N.E.			
Villa Jouar el Bawachek	**B	9	
AALEY, 900 m, 17 km S.E.			
Panorama	***A	64	55.36.08
Rond-Point	***B	68	55.08.03
Tanios	***B	115	—
Aley Al Kabir	***C	44	55.07.60
Montania	***C	63	55.11.64
and 4 hotels**, 18 hotels·*.			
AAJALTOUN, 900 m, 26 km N.E.			
Braidi	**B	20	95.02.24
Miramar	**B	30	95.02.27
Monte Bello	**B	41	95.02.32
Floridor	**C	16	—
AARAMOUN, 500 m, 17 km S.			
Villa Luna Rossa	**B	7	1
AINAB, 730 m, 28 km S.			
Pension Saint Charles	**D	14	57.53.17
AIN ZHALTA, 1090 m, 39 km S.E.			
Bellevue	**C	28	
Green Mountain	**C	9	16
Victoria	**C	31	1
AITOU, 950 m, 113 km N.E.			
Pension Aïtou	**A	7	7
BAABDAT, 850 m, 25 km E.			
Shalimar	***A	56	—
Colibri	***C	50	97.54.02
and 2 hotels **.			
BAALACHMAY, 1050 m, 22 km S.E.			
Esplanada	***A	66	56.05.20
and 1 hotel **C.			
BAALBEK, 1170 m, 85 km N.E.			
Alouette	***A	47	34.69.10
Palmyra	***C	41	1
and 1 hotel **, 5 hotels *.			
BÉCHARRÉ, 1450 m, 126 km N.E.			
Chebat	***B	40	67.02.70
and 2 hotels **, 1 hotel *.			
BEIT MÉRY, 740 m, 16 km E.			
Bustan (swimming pool).	****A	147	96.08.66
and 1 hotel **, 1 hotel *.			
BEYROUTH			
Beau Rivage, Ramlet Baida (swimming pool)	****A	94	30.31.20
Beirut Carlton, av. Gl. de Gaulle (swimming pool)	****A	144	30.02.40

*The ultra-modern swimming pool of Saint George's beach
receives the cream of Beirut society at apéritif time.
(Photo NCT.)*

Beirut International,			
av. Gl. de Gaulle (swimming pool)	****A	99	30.00.16
Bristol, rue Mme Curie	****A	162	35.14.00
Cadmos, rue Aïn Mreisseh	****A	113	29.77.10
Holiday Inn,			
rue Georges Picot (swimming pool)	****A	500	23.70.38
Martinez, rue Phoenicia	****A	133	23.73.60
Phoenicia,			
rue Fakhreddine (swimming pool)	****A	548	25.29.00
St Georges, Minet el Hosn	****A	104	22.05.60
Vendôme, Minet el Hosn	****A	125	29.22.80
Alcazar, Minet el Hosn	****B	80	23.13.40
Atlantic,			
Ramlet Baida (swimming pool)	****B	79	30.01.47
Commodore,			
rue de Lyon (swimming pool)	****B	148	35.04.00
Byblos, rue Georges Picot	****B	51	25.10.30
Cavalier, rue Hamra	****B	64	—
Continental,			
av. Gl de Gaulle (swimming pool)	****B	88	31.10.15
Excelsior,			
Minet el-Hosn (swimming pool)	****B	105	22.14.20
King's,			
rue de Grenade (swimming pool)	****B	136	29.75.01
Méditerranée, Ramlet Baïda	****B	100	—
Melkart,			
Ramlet Baida (swimming pool)	****B	105	30.69.10
Napoléon, rue Makdissis	****B	84	34.02.07
Pavillon, rue Hamra	****B	62	35.01.60
Riviera,			
av. de Paris (swimming pool)	****B	135	22.14.80
Rodin, Roustom Pacha	****B	75	22.34.22
and 35 hotels ***,			
17 hotels**, 29 hotels *.			

BHAMDOUN, 1140 m, 25 km S.E.			
Sémiramis	***C	62	56.02.76
and 4 hotels *.			

BHAMDOUN-GARE, 1075 m, 23 km S.E.			
Cheikh	****A	125	56.13.00
Karmah	****B	130	56.03.01
Shepherd's	****B	97	56.05.70
and 6 hotels ***, 7 hotels**, 19 hotels *.			

BHIRSAF, 960 m, 26 km E.			
Luxe	**C	15	—

BIKFAYA, 910 m, 25 km E.			
Amiriye al Jadid	***C	20	98.04.83
Amiriye	***C	38	98.04.82
and 3 hotels *.			

BMAKKINE, 700 m, 24 km S.E.			
Royal	***A	45	55.19.50
and 3 hotels **.			

BOLOGNIA, 1250 m, 33 km E.			
Bois de Boulogne	***A	64	99.08.05
Summer Palace (swimming pool)	***B	48	99.07.79
and 1 hotel **, 3 hotels *.			

How can one possibly not dream of relaxing in this splendid decor!
(Beirut's Bristol Hotel).
(Photo NCT - Yetenegian.)

BROUMMANA, 780 m, 20 km E.

Printania Palace (swimming pool)	****B	79	96.04.15
Garden	***C	45	96.05.79
and 25 hotels **.			

BTIKHNAY, 1000 m, 38 km E.

Villa El Mira	**D	12	123

BZOUMMAR, 920 m, 36 km N.E.

Bzoummâr	**A	86	31

CEDRES (les), 1840 m, 130 km N.E.

Le Chalet	***A	19	67.02.27
St Bernard	***C	25	67.80.24
Château-Blanc	**A	57	67.80.05
Mon Repos	**A	36	67.80.34
Rancho Grande	**A	55	67.80.01
Cortina	**C	27	67.80.31
La Cabane	**D	13	67.80.06
and 3 hotels *.			

CHIYAH, 600 m, 5 km S.

Coral Beach (swimming pool)	****B	81	37.72.00
Sands of Lebanon (swimming pool)	****B	171	—
and 2 hotels **			

CHTAURA, 910 m, 44 km E.

Chtaura Park Hôtel (swimming pool)	****E	87	84.09.97
Massabki	***C	27	84.07.55
and 4 hotels **, 5 hotels *.			

DALHAMIYÉ (Ed), 400 m, 30 km S.

Dalhamiyé Country Club (swimming pool)	***A	12	53.05.82

DEIR EL-QAMAR, 790 m, 40 km S.

Hnoud	**C	25	50.51.05
Villa Deir El-Qamar	**C	14	50.50.79

DHOUR ECH-CHOUEIR, 1250 m, 27 km E.

Kassouf	***A	62	99.05.01
and 5 hotels **, 4 hotels *.			

EHDEN, 1470 m, 124 km N.E.

Belmont	***B	46	67.30.91
and 2 hotels **, 2 hotels *.			

FAITROUN, 1200 m, 33 km N.E.

Massaad	**A	58	95.02.86
Faïtroun	**B	32	95.00.09
Nassri	**C	22	95.02.04

FALOUGHA, 1250 m, 35 km   E.

Park	**B	48	3
Saadé	**C	28	9
and 8 hotels *.			

FARAIYA, 1310 m, 46 km N.E.

Fâraiya el Mzaar (swimming pool)	****B	77	24.00.66
San Antonio	***C	124	24.77.21
Bader	**B	23	3
Boule de Neige	**C	52	—
Grand Hôtel	**C	33	4
and 6 hotels *.			

*Oriental architecture designs, the fabulous
residence of Mr. Pharaon...*

HADETH EJ-JOBBÉ, 1440 m, 99 km N.E.

Barakat	**B	30	67.71.34
Bassile	**C	29	67.70.03
Chedraoui	**C	25	67.72.14
Hitti	**C	15	67.70.32
Mtill el Mchalka	**C	15	67.70.32

and 1 hotel *.

HALAT, 100 m, 32 km N.

Quatre Saisons (motel) (swimming pool)	**B	17	93.36.16

HAMMANA, 1100 m, 33 km E.

Chaghour	**B	26	57.00.07
Aïn El-Hassa	**C	33	57.00.15
Touriste	**C	19	57.02.55
Villa New Royal	**C	8	57.01.53

and 2 hotels *.

HASROUN EJ-JDIDE, 1380 m, 105 km N.E.

Semaani	**B	20	67.50.10
Palace	**B	24	67.51.15

and 1 hotel*

HAZMIYE, 50 m, 6 km S.E.

Confort	**A	35	28.13.15

JBAIL (BYBLOS), 10 m, 37 km N.

Byblos-sur-mer (private beach)	***A	36	94.03.56
Ahiram	**A	25	94.04.44
Fishing-Club (private beach)	**B	15	94.02.13

JDITA, 1010 m, 44 km E.

Khater	**A	35	84.06.59

JEZZINE, 950 m, 73 km S.

Haddad	**C	26	4

and 4 hotels *.

JOURET ET TERMOSS, 950 m, 40 km N.E.

Adonis,	**B	37	3
Saint Paul	**B	31	11

KARTABA, 1170 m, 57 km N.E.

Rivoli	**A	22	—

and 6 hotels *.

KFAR ZEBIANE, 1250 m, 44 km N.E.

Pension Is'hak	**C	10	36
Salamé	**C	19	12

and 1 hotel *.

KFOUR (EL), 830 m, 35 km N.E.

Pension Saïf	**B	13	4

and 2 hotels *

KHALDÉ, seaside (near Beirut Airport)

Libanon Beach (swimming pool)	****B	75	43.03.49
Mirador (swimming pool)	****B	111	43.04.00
Deauville (swimming pool)	***A	98	43.08.88
Marrouche (swimming pool)	***A	58	43.08.73
La Siesta (motel) (swimming pool)	***A	124	43.05.51
Château de Versailles (swimming pool)	***C	56	43.08.70

The Alcazar Hotel lounge in Beirut
(Photo NCT - Yetenegian.)

KINCHARA, 1070 m, 30 km E.

Ain el Samidiyeh	**A	14	99.06.87
Dar el Zaghalil	**D	9	99.06.04

KORNAYEL, 1160 m, 35 km E.

Palais des Pins	**C	19	11
and 2 hotels *.			

LAKLOUK, 1920 m, 69 km N.E.

Shangrilla	***A	57	23.50.44
Nirvana (swimming pool)	***C	51	23.50.44

MAAMELTEIN, seaside, 23 km N.

Montemar (private beach)	***B	37	93.19.96
Saint-Gilles (swimming pool and private beach)	**C	15	93.04.20
and 6 hotels *.			

MEYROUBA, 1300 m, 38 km N.E.

Aïn el Jern	**A	30	5
Kessrouane	**A	29	10
and 5 hotels *.			

NAAS, 1000 m, 27 km E.

Granada	**A	47	98.02.34
Merryland	**A	26	98.03.90
Grand Hôtel Naas	**A	32	98.01.13
Saint Michel	**A	53	98.02.23
Naas	**B	42	98.01.13

NAHR AL-KALB, (SOUK MOSBEH),
seaside, 15 km N.

Holiday Beach Hôtel (swimming pool and private beach)	****B	152	93.06.10

QANAT BAKICH, 1775 m,
new winter sports station.

Qanat Bakich	**A	10	24.50.41
Villa Bakich	**A	70	24.83.72

RAYFOUN, 1050 m, 28 km N.E.

Saint Roch	****B	100	95.00.76
and 3 hotels **, 2 hotels *.			

SAIDA, seaside, 43 km S.
4 hotels* (about 28 rooms.)

SANNINE, 1650 m, 51 km E.

Monte Sannine	**B	16	5
Villa Capitale	**B	14	146
and 5 hotels *.			

SIR ED-DANNIYÉ, 900 m, 111 km N.E.

Loubnan	**B	60	66.50.47
Sir el Kabir	**B	53	66.50.97
Sir Palace	**B	25	66.52.02
and 6 hotels *.			

SOFAR, 1275 m, 26 km S.E.

Château Bernina	****B	41	56.18.30
Grand Casino	***A	75	—

Rich and sobre, the lounge of Lebanon's Casino in Maameltein.
(Photo NCT - Yetenegian.)

SOUK AL-GHARB, 760 m, 22 km S.E.

Hajjar	****B	97	57.55.31
and 3 hotels **, 1 hotel *			

SOUR, seaside, 85 km S.

Resthouse			

TABARJA, seaside, 24 km N.

Tabarja Beach (swimming pool and private beach)	****B	225	93.03.82

TRIPOLI, seaside, 86 km N.

Al Mountazah	***A	37	62.66.88
Royal Al Kabir	**B	19	62.27.94
Palace	**D	14	62.22.57
and 21 hotels *.			

ZAHLÉ, 1000 m, 52 km E.

Kadri	***C	69	
Pension Casino	**B	9	82.16.28
and 12 hotels *.			

*In old Sidon, the modern Saïda, one enjoys sitting at a table in
the Rest-House by the sea-side.
(Photo NCT - Yetenegian.)*

lebanon
today

EDITIONS ⧓ **JEUNE AFRIQUE**

translated by	colin j. norris
photographs	by the author except when otherwise credited
layout by	aldo de silva

© 1974
EDITIONS JEUNE AFRIQUE
51, avenue des ternes - 75017 paris
all rights reserved

printed in holland
dépôt légal 2ᵉ trimestre 1974
nᵒ d'éditeur 1120/1
ISBN 2-85258-004-7

in the
same
series

by jean hureau ■ la tunisie aujourd'hui
■ le maroc aujourd'hui
■ la corse aujourd'hui
■ l'espagne aujourd'hui
■ l'iran aujourd'hui
■ la provence et la côte d'azur aujourd'hui
■ la bretagne aujourd'hui
by louis doucet ■ la grèce aujourd'hui
by rené bauchar ■ l'afrique noire et l'océan indien
francophones aujourd'hui *

* All the above titles are available
in french and in german.
An english version
being printed
Already published :
"Iran today"